US AND UK UNEMPLOYMENT BETWEEN THE WARS: A DOLEFUL STORY

US AND UK UNEMPLOYMENT BETWEEN THE WARS: A DOLEFUL STORY

Dan Benjamin
*Clemson University,
Clemson, S. Carolina*

Kent Matthews
*Cardiff Business School,
Cardiff*

IEA

**Institute of Economic Affairs
1992**

First published in May 1992
by
THE INSTITUTE OF ECONOMIC AFFAIRS
2 Lord North Street, Westminster, London SW1P 3LB

Hobart Paperback 31

ISSN 0309-1783
ISBN 0-255 36305-2

The Institute gratefully acknowledges financial support for its publications programme and other work from a generous benefaction by the late Alec and Beryl Warren.

All the Institute's publications seek to further its objective of promoting the advancement of learning, by research into economic and political science, by education of the public therein, and by the dissemination of ideas, research and the results of research in these subjects. The views expressed are those of the authors, not of the IEA, which has no corporate view.

Printed in Great Britain by
Goron Pro-Print Co. Ltd., Lancing, W. Sussex

Filmset in 'Berthold' Times Roman 11 on 12 point

CONTENTS

LIST OF TABLES

LIST OF CHARTS

FOREWORD

Colin Robinson
Editorial Director,
Institute of Economic Affairs

MEMORIES OF THE INTER-WAR PERIOD, both in Britain and the United States, focus on industrial depression and on unemployment which was very high by previous and subsequent standards. Not surprisingly, the distressing experience of the thirties in America and both the twenties and thirties in Britain has left long-lasting marks on economic policy. Events seemed, at the time, to demonstrate that self-correcting tendencies in the economy are weak so that positive government action is required both to steer the economy and to move individual markets in 'socially desirable' directions.

Economic policy recommendations, stemming from inter-war experience, re-inforced the natural desire of politicians and bureaucrats to extend their spheres of influence: the power of the state grew on both sides of the Atlantic and has not been noticeably rolled back even in recent times. Although the more naïve demand-management views of followers of Keynes (rather than of Keynes himself) have long been discredited, economic policies are still influenced by perceptions of the lessons which can be drawn from the inter-war years: many politicians remain slaves to the views of defunct economists.

Because of the influence of inter-war experiences on policy-making to this day, it is important to draw the proper lessons from those experiences. What does the inter-war period have to tell us about the reasons for persistently high unemployment? Despite our advantage of hindsight, it is a difficult question to answer. The period is not a promising one for econometric analysis, both because it is too short to generate the long time-series econometricians like to handle and because the required statistics are poor or even, in some cases, non-existent. Consequently, analysts have to resort to unsatisfactory expedients such as interpolating data or using series which are rather poor substitutes for those they would prefer to have.

Despite the difficulties, there has been a revival of interest in discovering reasons why unemployment was so high between the wars. In this paper, Dan Benjamin and Kent Matthews make an important contribution to this revived debate, laying great emphasis—as IEA authors generally do—on the incentives which influence people in making choices. In this case, the relevant choice is between working and not working which is influenced by the perceived costs and benefits attaching to the chosen course of action. Consequently, as they point out, a reduction in the costs of not working is likely to lead to more unemployment.

Benjamin and Matthews begin their argument (in Chapter 2) from the paradox of high unemployment in Britain between the wars. Though the statistics are far from ideal, it appears that real income increased at about the same rate (2 per cent per annum on average) between 1920 and 1938 as during the 50 years before the First World War. Yet, inter-war unemployment averaged 14 per cent compared with less than 4 per cent in the earlier period. In the United States, there is a different though related puzzle. Even though real output rose sharply from the mid-thirties onwards, employment failed to recover.

The case made by the authors to resolve the paradoxes and puzzles of inter-war unemployment rests, as they point out in Chapter 3, on one simple proposition: 'lowering the cost of any activity will induce people to engage in more of that activity'. The relevant application of this proposition (the downward-sloping demand curve, in economists' language) is that, if the cost of being unemployed is reduced, then more people will choose to be unemployed. They go on to provide econometric and other evidence that the unemployment compensation schemes, introduced in Britain from 1920 onwards and from the mid-thirties in the United States, were one of the principal reasons for the substantial increase in unemployment. There was more unemployment than there would otherwise have been because some people chose not to work, or searched longer between jobs, or exploited the regulations (as under the British inter-war 'OXO' schemes) so as to claim benefit. As Benjamin and Matthews acknowledge, their views bear some resemblance to those expressed by Rueff, Pigou and Cannan in the 1920s and 1930s, all of whom believed (albeit on evidence collected less carefully) that changes to unemployment insurance were a factor in rising unemployment.

In the authors' words, '. . . the inter-war unemployment insurance system importantly shaped the unemployment histories of every nook and cranny of Britain' (page 110). They argue that time-series and cross-section evidence for Britain suggests that the insurance system may have raised the unemployment rate by at least five to eight percentage points. Effects of the US system (which was instituted later) seem to have been less; nevertheless, the incentives which existed under the US scheme appear to provide an explanation of why unemployment fell so slowly during the output recovery of the late 1930s.

Benjamin and Matthews conclude (Chapter 6) by drawing some lessons for the future, the most important of which is that policy-makers need to understand the consequences of their actions. The story of the inter-war years shows, in their view, that policy-makers '. . . did not fully understand the consequences of their actions, and so not only administered more of the same, but also more of just about everything—so as to do something, anything' (page 152). They illustrate the lessons which can be derived from their analysis by reference to the 'liberalisation' of the British unemployment benefit system from 1966 onwards (which was accompanied by rising unemployment, especially of juveniles). As they make plain, they do not advocate the abolition of social insurance. But they do ask that policy-makers examine the costs of their actions. Otherwise, their 'remedies' may be worse than the diseases they seek to cure.

The views expressed in this *Hobart Paperback* are, of course, those of the authors and not those of the Institute (which has no corporate view), its Trustees, its Directors or its Advisers. The Institute publishes it as a lively and stimulating contribution to debate, not only about inter-war unemployment but about economic policy today.

April 1992 COLIN ROBINSON

AUTHORS' INTRODUCTION

THIS IS THE PAGE on which the baton is passed, from author to reader. It is also the point at which we confess the awful truth: all of the blame but none of the credit belongs to us—or so it seems when it comes to acknowledging the debts we have accumulated in writing what follows.

The origin of our research on the United Kingdom is pure serendipity—an off-hand remark by a Swedish Count then residing in California, one Axel Leijonhufvud, Professor of Economics at University of California, Los Angeles. The remark made in 1970 was roughly: 'Whatever Keynes's *General Theory* might be, it is not an explanation of unemployment in inter-war Britain'. This led to a series of papers by Benjamin and Levis A. Kochin of the University of Washington, work that provided much of the underpinnings of the findings we report here. Professor Patrick Minford of the University of Liverpool arranged and provided the funding through the ESRC Liverpool Macroeconomic Research Project, for Benjamin and Kochin to visit Liverpool in 1981 and a further visit by Benjamin in 1987. Professor Charles Nelson of the University of Washington and Professor Michael T. Maloney of Clemson University, also provided support that helped make these visits possible. Professor Maloney and Professor Roger Meiners, Director of the Center for Policy Studies at Clemson, assisted in arranging a visit by Matthews to Clemson in 1986, and a further trip in 1988. Both trips were funded by the Nuffield Foundation. It was on the first of these trips that the present work began. The Center for Policy

Studies at Clemson has subsequently provided financial support for Benjamin's research.

Our research on the American experience is based on the seminal work conducted by Professor John Wallis of the University of Maryland over the past decade. The data we use were provided by Professor Wallis; they were originally compiled by Wallis with the financial assistance of the US Department of Labor and the National Science Foundation, and even now are in the process of revision by him (some of this data was published by Wallis in *Explorations in Economic History*, Vol. 26, No. 1, January 1989). Although we believe our findings represent a substantial improvement over the prior state of knowledge, the definitive answers about this period will no doubt have to wait until Wallis has completed his researches.

Our thanks go to Arthur Seldon for encouraging us to publish our research findings in the form of a Hobart Paperback. Special thanks go to Mike Solly for reading and commenting on various redrafts of the manuscript. We also acknowledge the helpful comments of two anonymous referees.

Our debt to Patrick Minford extends far beyond the acknowledgements noted above. The financial, intellectual, and personal support that he has provided over the years has transcended generosity—but that will come as little surprise to those who know him. We also owe special thanks to our respective wives, who repeatedly packed their bags (and ours) as we migrated back and forth across the Atlantic.

D.K.B.

K.G.P.M.

THE AUTHORS

DANIEL K. BENJAMIN is Professor of Economics and Senior Research Scholar at Clemson University, South Carolina. He was educated at the University of Virginia and the University of California, Los Angeles, where he was a National Science Foundation Fellow. He has taught at the Universities of California at Santa Barbara, Washington in Seattle, and Clemson.

In addition to serving as a staff economist with the President's Council of Economic Advisors, Professor Benjamin has been Deputy Assistant Secretary of Labor, and served as Chief of Staff at the US Department of Labor, and principal policy advisor to the Secretary of Labor.

Benjamin has been a National Fellow at Stanford University, a Visiting Scholar at the American Enterprise Institute, and a Visiting Distinguished Scholar at the University of Liverpool. He is the author or editor of seven books, and numerous scholarly articles. He has been an Associate Editor of *Economic Inquiry*, and served on the Executive Committee of the Western Economic Association, and the Advisory Board of the Pacific Institute.

KENT MATTHEWS is Senior Lecturer in Economics at the Cardiff Business School, and Visiting Professor, Catholic University of Louvain, Belgium. He was formerly a Lecturer in Monetary Economics, University of Liverpool, 1978-89, and

Principal Forecaster with the Liverpool Research Group in Macro-economics, 1980-89. He was Visiting Fellow at the Center for Policy Studies, Clemson University, in July-August 1986, where this work began. He took degrees at the London School of Economics and Political Science, Birkbeck College, and the University of Liverpool.

ACKNOWLEDGEMENTS

We are grateful to the Nuffield Foundation and to the ESRC (B01250028) for financial support.

D.K.B.
K.G.P.M.

1

HARD TIMES

Introduction

THE EMERGENCE of prolonged high unemployment is the best remembered fact of the years between the two World Wars. From 1921 to 1938 unemployment in Great Britain averaged 14 per cent and never fell below 9·5 per cent. Indeed, in every year between 1921 and 1938 the unemployment rate was higher than it had been in all except two years prior to 1921. In America, the effervescence of the 'Roaring Twenties' was crushed by the aptly-christened 'Great Depression', as the unemployment rate soared to 25 per cent. And despite the best efforts of Roosevelt's 'New Deal', unemployment refused to drop below 15 per cent, as millions of Americans were forced to rely on the state for their very survival. Save for the onset of the Second World War, it appeared that full employment might never return to the shores of the North Atlantic.

The hard times spread far beyond mere labour force statistics. Among those people who lived it, the inter-war period evokes vivid memories of hunger marches, soup kitchens, dole queues, and red banners proclaiming 'the right to work'. The enduring image of the era is one of poverty and deprivation caused by the denial of work, and the struggles of ordinary people against the ravages of unemployment, captured in the poignant tales of the Hardcastles of Salford and the Joad family of Oklahoma.[1]

[1] *Cf.* Walter Greenwood's novel, *Love on the Dole* (1933), subsequently refashioned as a play, and John Steinbeck's powerful novel, *The Grapes of Wrath*, respectively.

Although separated by the vast, grey expanse of the Atlantic, those who experienced the hardships were irrevocably united in their stoic endurance of the 'Hungry Thirties'.

In Britain, the persistently high rate of unemployment was the principal topic of inter-war economics, and its solution the principal issue of inter-war politics. Indeed, the 'army of one million unemployed' that emerged after the First World War and stood watch on the eve of the Second World War, immutably defined the intellectual and political debates of the era. In both arenas, the proper rôle of the British government became transformed from defender of the Empire to provider of last resort. Ultimately, the trauma of this standing army shaped not only the views of the generation that lived it, but impressed itself upon the attitudes of later generations in a way that has not—as yet—wholly disappeared.

The chaos, deprivation, and despair of the 1930s wrought changes in the American psyche equalling any before or since. The era recast the American view of the rôle government could—and should—play in society. Prior to the Great Depression, government was perceived as at best an instrument of an individualistic society, and at worst an impediment to the free expression of that individualism. Within less than a decade, the American people came to see government as saviour, as an entity unto itself, capable of feats unattainable by other means, including their own. Government action had rescued America from ruin, and thus could—and should—be the first line of defence against future threats, real or imagined. This mental transformation of government from servant to partner—and sometimes master—remains even today a hallmark of the American social, economic, and political milieu.

1. Paradoxes

The inter-war period was, and remains, the object of intense scrutiny and debate. At the most elemental level, the reason for this interest is simple: the economic turbulence that struck both Britain and America exceeded any witnessed in those nations before or since. Britain experienced two of the sharpest recessions of its history, and the unemployment rate hit—and remained lodged at—record levels. The depression that enveloped America was literally unprecedented; it pushed the unemployment rate to four times the normal level, and left the economy a shattered ruin of its former self. The economic upheaval of the era created social and intellectual trauma that was, and remains, inescapable.

Just as importantly, the inter-war years were years of chaos in the definitive sense of that word: 'extreme confusion or disorder'. The unemployment that gripped Britain for two decades rose unbidden from an unknown source, seemingly impervious to human action and reason, and beyond the realm of prior human experience. It was inexplicable and implacable. And even after Lord Keynes's theory of deficient aggregate demand appeared to bring order where none had been, a new puzzle arose: a re-examination of the historical record showed that the unemployment experience of the period had not fitted the mould cast for it by the savant. Despite two recessions, the growth rate of real income, the extent of business expansion, and even the level of investment were all normal by historical standards. How had deficient demand harvested the army of the unemployed, even while leaving the fruits of labour and capital unscathed? It was a question left unanswered long after Keynes's death.

The paradoxes of America were rather different. After a sharp but short post-First World War recession, America began eight years of virtually unalloyed economic success. The 'Roaring Twenties' brought industrial expansion, low unemployment, and stable prices—heady stuff in the face of the miseries gripping Britain. The sea change came abruptly in October 1929 as the bottom fell out of the American stock market; within months, the foundations of the economy had followed it downward. Between 1929 and 1933 both real income and the price level fell by a third, as the unemployment rate soared to 25 per cent of the work-force. The frontier-hardened Americans had known tough times, but nothing like this. A people self-perceived as the champions of progress and rising prosperity found themselves astride an economic system reduced to rubble, with no idea of what had happened, and little notion of what to do about it.

Roosevelt offered the New Deal, and grateful Americans accepted it with gusto. Yet even eight years later, the unemployment rate was still in double-digits, and millions of its citizens remained wards of Roosevelt's make-work programmes. Keynes's theories solved the puzzle of *what* had happened (deficient demand), and Friedman and Schwartz ultimately unravelled the puzzle of *why* it happened (misguided central bank policy). Yet both left unanswered the final paradox: As America girded itself for war, why were so many Americans still so dependent on the government for their livelihood?

2. Solutions?

On one point there has been no debate: the economies on both sides of the Atlantic were subject to deflationary shocks during the inter-war years. The emergence of unemployment in response to such shocks was no more of a mystery to the classical economists of the period than it is today. Thus, when monetary restriction was begun in 1920, few contemporary economists were surprised to see the unemployment rates in Britain and America rise rapidly. Cannan, Fisher, Keynes and others were cognisant that few prices were perfectly flexible; as a result, they recognised that a general deflation would be accompanied by an industrial crisis. A temporary increase in unemployment was simply the price to be paid if the post-war inflation was to be reversed. The recession played itself out quickly in America, as unemployment returned to normal levels with the onset of recovery. Events in Britain soon turned puzzling, however, for despite a vigorous economic expansion, the unemployment rate refused to fall below 10 per cent.

The refusal of unemployment to co-operate with accepted theories led the classical economists to search for real supply factors that could account for the events about them. Many quickly focussed on the behaviour of trade unions, combined with the operation of the unemployment insurance scheme (established just before the War and greatly expanded in 1920). The story was simple: emboldened by the insurance scheme's subsidy to unemployment, the unions were bargaining for supra-normal wages, which in turn led to lay-offs and (financially comfortable) unemployment for their members. Critics quickly attacked this view, pointing out that the explanation foundered on the facts. Union membership in Britain was in decline, not ascendancy; why had the unions not taken advantage of their clearly superior pre-war bargaining position? Moreover, the evidence showed that unemployment was highest in industries where wage gains had been the lowest, a finding directly opposed to what would be expected if the unions were at the root of the problem. As far as unemployment insurance was concerned, the theory seemed to imply the emergence of long-term unemployment, when in fact it was short-term unemployment that blossomed. 'Short-time' working arrangements, in which employees rotated between regular spells of work and unemployment, were the norm after 1921. Besides, it seemed unpleasantly hard-hearted to propose that workers were voluntarily choosing unemployment in the face of record-length dole queues.

Return to the Gold Standard

The chief competing explanation for Britain's failure to achieve full employment during the 1920s focussed on the government's decision to return to gold at the pre-war parity.[1] The wartime inflation meant that a major downward adjustment in the post-war price level was required to achieve consistency with the desired terms of trade. The monetary restriction of 1920-21 had clearly begun this process. And since the adjustment appeared to be not yet complete by resumption in 1925, the deflationary pressures of the first half of the decade were simply carried over to the second half. This explanation had great appeal in the principal exporting nation of the world. Yet it left a pivotal question unanswered: Since pre-war parity was widely known to be the centre-piece of the government's economic policy, why were prices and wages steadfastly failing to adjust to the requisite equilibrium levels?

When a fresh gale of deflation swept out of America in 1930, unemployment soared above 20 per cent for the first time in Britain's history. The government's response was draconian: it sharply cut unemployment benefits and eligibility, and abandoned gold. The economy began a sharp rebound, yet unemployment still did not return to normal levels. When Keynes finally proposed a theory in which unemployment equilibria were possible in the face of deficient demand, his colleagues quickly took up the cause. And when the demand stimulus produced by the Second World War quickly brought unemployment back to normal levels, there was no doubt that both problem and cause

[1] Prior to the outbreak of the First World War, the pound sterling was convertible into gold. In principle, a hundred pounds could be exchanged for a hundred gold sovereigns. Because the gold content of the sovereign was 486 per cent of the US gold dollar, the par value of the pound was fixed at $4·86.

had been correctly identified. Unemployment need never be feared again.

1929 Crash Ends Roaring Twenties

In America, economists and politicians alike had been basking in the glow of the Roaring Twenties, largely unconcerned with the misery plaguing their British counterparts. Thus, when first recession and then depression overwhelmed the economy after the stock market crash, policy-makers and their advisers were unprepared for the chaos. Some perceived that the Federal Reserve's 1929 efforts to quell stock market speculation had been perhaps too vigorous. Others argued that the nation's protectionist sentiments, capped by the ruinous Smoot-Hawley tariffs of 1930, had fatally disrupted world trade. But as the depression deepened, the Federal Reserve silenced its critics with compelling pleas that matters were out of its hands.

Moreover, it soon became evident that even prohibitive trade measures could not produce a 50 per cent decline in industrial production or a 25 per cent unemployment rate. A handful of influential economists, in a move that at least partly presaged Keynes, urged the government to undertake large-scale government spending. Upon his election in 1933, Roosevelt embodied this advice in his New Deal programmes, and recovery soon began. Even so, by 1936 unemployment was still 15 per cent, and four million Americans were dependent on government relief programmes for their livelihood. With propitious timing, the publication of *The General Theory* not only validated Roosevelt's efforts, but warranted more of the same. The Second World War provided both the impetus for the spending and, it seemed, the proof of its efficacy. In short order, the Keynesian Revolution became a *fait accompli.*

3. Questions

The experience of the first two decades after the Second World War re-affirmed the view of politicians and economists that the key to perpetual prosperity had indeed been found. Britain and the United States both enjoyed full employment, economic growth, and low inflation. Demand management evolved into 'fine-tuning', and it seemed as though the time was near when the macro-economies of the world could simply be put on autopilot, allowing the policy-makers and their advisers to search for other problems to solve.

In the background, however, an intellectual counter-revolution was quietly gathering strength. Spearheaded by the work of Milton Friedman, the emerging neo-classical view suggested a radical re-interpretation of both history and policy. Friedman and Schwartz (1963) directly addressed the inter-war period in the United States, compiling an impressive body of evidence. Their findings implied that the received view of the American experience had got things backwards. Monetary policy had not been powerless in the face of deflationary forces; on the contrary, it was monetary policy that had been responsible for the Great Depression, and mainly monetary policy that had brought about recovery. Subsequent work by Alchian, Phelps, Lucas and others argued forcefully that despite the evident potency of monetary policy, it was a beast not easily tamed—at least not for the purposes of fine-tuning national economies. The economic turbulence of the 1970s—rampant inflation accompanied by unemployment nearing inter-war levels—provided compelling evidence that demand management was no simple task, and that supply factors were far more pivotal than allowed for in received theory. The pioneering work of Friedman and Schwartz had resolved many of the mysteries of the American experience during the inter-war years. Yet, as even they admitted, one crucial puzzle remained. Unemployment in the United States during the late 1930s seemed too high to be accounted for, given the vigorous recovery evident elsewhere in the economy:

> '. . . the most notable feature of the recovery after 1933 was not its rapidity but its incompleteness. Throughout the revival, unemployment remained large. Even at its cyclical peak in 1937, seasonally adjusted unemployment was 5·9 million . . . out of a labour force of nearly 54 million' (Friedman and Schwartz, 1963, p. 493).

Then, too, there remained the paradox of Britain, viewed within the context of the neo-classical paradigm. Although there had been two recessions during the inter-war period, Britain's 1931 departure from gold had insulated the economy from the Great Depression. Overall, real income growth in Britain during the inter-war years equalled or exceeded historical norms, and yet the unemployment rate averaged 14 per cent. No one presumed that 'search' unemployment[1] could account for the facts, nor did it seem possible that long-term contracts could have prevented the adjustment to equilibrium for two decades. The unemployment experience of inter-war Britain was simply not consistent with the other known facts.

During the late 1970s, research appeared which suggested explanations for both the American experience of the late 1930s and the British experience of the entire inter-war period. Darby (1976) argued that much of the seeming excess unemployment in America after 1933 was simply mislabelled. Many of the individuals counted as being unemployed were actually working on New Deal relief projects, most notably those operating under the Works Progress Administration. Darby argued that these individuals should be counted as gainfully employed in government jobs, rather than as unemployed. Once this 're-count' was performed, Darby concluded, the mystery of high US unemployment during the late 1930s disappeared.

The British Paradox Explained

Benjamin and Kochin (1979a) took aim at the British experience. Conceptually, they divided the supra-normal unemployment of the inter-war period into two components. In 1920-21 and again in 1930-31, they argued, the British economy was subjected to monetary restrictions, resulting in increases in unemployment that were easily fathomed in classical terms, and even better appreciated when viewed in the light of neo-classical theory. They attributed the excess unemployment of the late 1920s and 1930s to an equally classical source: in 1920 the British government had greatly expanded the scope and increased the generosity of the unemployment insurance scheme. Combined with a relaxation of the traditional safeguards against the 'abuse' of unemployment insurance, these changes presented employer and employee with the opportunity to take advantage of a huge subsidy to unemployment. In its simplest terms, the hypothesis of Benjamin and Kochin is but an application of the economist's Law of Demand: government policy lowered the private cost of being unemployed, and the British people chose to consume more unemployment.

[1] Those who are not undertaking paid work but who are in the process of searching for work.

The revisionist explanations for the inter-war experience offered by Darby and by Benjamin and Kochin were immediately subjected to attack. The most telling critique of Darby was that his work consisted largely of simply *asserting* that government relief recipients should be re-classified as *bona fide* government workers. Nowhere does Darby ask or answer the counter-factual question: If relief recipients had not been able to avail themselves of the New Deal programmes, would they actually have found work in the private economy? The principal lasting critique of Benjamin and Kochin is that, despite the impressive cross-sectional evidence they present, their time-series evidence is marred by the rudimentary reduced-form model they employ.

Oddly, the subsequent intellectual response to these re-interpretations of the British and American inter-war experiences has followed widely divergent paths. In some quarters, Darby's 'mislabelling' hypothesis has been largely accepted as being self-evident. Elsewhere, it has been equally as fully dismissed as mere speculation. But except for the papers by Kesselman and Savin (1978) and Wallis and Benjamin (1981), little published research has attempted to answer the central counter-factual question left unanswered by Darby. By contrast, the work by Benjamin and Kochin has spawned a plethora of papers on the rôle of the dole in inter-war Britain. As the evidence has accumulated, the central focus of the debate has shifted, from *whether* the insurance system raised unemployment in inter-war Britain, to *how much* additional unemployment the system produced. Significantly, the debate over history has ultimately helped shape both the debate and the course of contemporary policy.

4. Lessons

The eminent philosopher George Santayana wrote that 'Those who forget the lessons of history are doomed to repeat them'.[1] Thus it is that the present work, narrowly cast as a treatise on economic history, is in a broader sense a guide to current action. Our goal here is thus threefold. First, we seek to present a concise vision of the current state of knowledge on the inter-war

[1] George Santayana, *The Life of Reason*, Vol. 1: *Reason in Common Sense*, 1905-06, extracted from *Bartletts Familiar Quotations*, ed. M. Beck, 15th edition revised and enlarged, Boston: Little and Brown, 1980.

experience. We do not pretend to be encyclopaedic. There is little that can be added, for example, to improve upon the work of Friedman and Schwartz and others on the course of monetary policy during this period. So we simply take this work as a given, extracting from it the salient facts required for our story, whose focus is on unravelling the unemployment puzzles of the period.

Secondly, we hope to resolve—or at least sharpen the debate on—the questions that remain unanswered despite the extensive research published over the past decade or so. For America, it seems to us that the issue can be cast quite simply: Did Roosevelt's New Deal programmes pull individuals out of private employment? Or did the programmes simply provide the unemployed with a source of income when no alternative was available? The new evidence we present here implies that it is the first question rather than the second which must be answered in the affirmative.

For Britain, the issues are twofold. First, is it possible, within the context of a more complete model of the economy, to extract useful information about inter-war unemployment from the meagre time-series data that are available? Secondly, does the extraordinary impact of the British unemployment insurance system during the inter-war years have lessons for the conduct of policy in less extraordinary times? We find the answer 'yes' is appropriate for both of these questions.

Our final goal is thus to enumerate both the scientific and policy lessons of the inter-war unemployment experience. There are several strands to each, but one that is common to both, and so worthy of emphasis at this point. The story that we tell here is one that was advanced more than 60 years ago, in the heat of the events we describe. Numerous inter-war economists argued that, although aggregate demand shocks initiated the unemployment of the early 1920s and 1930s, the unemployment of inter-war Britain was importantly due to the operation of the insurance system. In the United States, critics of the New Deal complained, in part, that Roosevelt's relief programmes were hampering the return of individuals to private employment. In both countries these views were rejected, at least partly because they portrayed a story that few politicians or economists *wanted* to hear. It was simply too hard-hearted to think of people responding to incentives, when it was self-evident that *something had to be done.*

But because the story was rejected, the Santayanaian inevitable occurred. Post-war policy-makers, most notably in Britain, eventually had the opportunity to make the choices confronted during the inter-war years. Blind to the lessons of history, they repeated their mistakes. In the mid-1960s in Britain, unemployment benefits were liberalised as they had been liberalised four decades earlier. As before, workers and employers responded to the system's incentives; and as before, higher unemployment was the result. Once again, policy-makers and their advisers rejected what they saw (or perhaps simply did not see it), spurning the truth in favour of a fiction that was distinctly more palatable; and once again, nearly two decades of policy confusion was the result. The tie that binds past and present is thus one of stark simplicity. There are many grounds on which policy battles may be fought, but when they are fought on the foundations of ignorance, to the victor will belong the spoils.

2

THE INTER-WAR ECONOMY

Introduction

THE INTER-WAR PERIOD—the years between the two World Wars—has long been a source of concern and debate among English-speaking peoples on both sides of the Atlantic. In only two years from 1855, when historical statistics began, up until 1920, was the unemployment rate as high as it was in every year from 1921 to 1938. The persistently high rate of unemployment in inter-war Britain has long dominated discussions of this era: it was the principal topic of inter-war British economics, and its solution was the principal issue of inter-war British politics. The 'army of one million unemployed', which emerged soon after the First World War and stood watch on the eve of the Second World War, is perhaps the best remembered feature of this period. Moreover, the trauma of this standing army impressed itself upon the attitude of more than one generation in a way that has not, as yet, wholly disappeared.

In the United States, the inter-war period is generally viewed as comprising two inexplicably contradictory régimes. After a brief post-war recession in 1920-21, the remainder of the 1920s—the so-called 'Roaring Twenties'—has been seen as a halcyon era in American economic history. The rapid economic growth of these years, combined with low unemployment and negligible inflation, has been viewed as being in stark contrast to the British experience during that decade—and an even harsher counterpoint to what was to follow in America.

The 'economic miracle' of America in the 1920s ended abruptly with the stock market crash of October 1929, which soon deepened into the Great Depression: between 1929 and 1933 both real income and the price level fell by a third, as the unemployment rate soared to 25 per cent of the work-force. Moreover, despite the best efforts of Roosevelt's New Deal programmes, unemployment in America suddenly proved as intractable as in Britain. Even by the end of the decade, the unemployment rate refused to move below 15 per cent of the work-force. But for the onset of the Second World War, it appeared that the full employment enjoyed in the 1920s might never again be attained.

Our purpose in this chapter is simple: we seek to 'debunk' widely held views of the inter-war economies of Great Britain and the United States. The 'stylised facts' that have dominated popular discussions and policy debates focussed on this period have grossly overshadowed equally important but less well recognised features of the era. In demonstrating this proposition, we hope to show that:

(i) the widely perceived *differences* between the British and American experiences of the inter-war years are much smaller than it might seem; but also that

(ii) the commonly held opinions on *similarities* between the economies of the two countries are equally misleading.

This discussion will set the stage for the ensuing chapters, where we develop the reasoning and evidence that enable us to resolve the remaining paradoxes of the era.

1. Britain Between the Wars

(a) The Historical Record

Great Britain emerged from the First World War faced with a fundamental conundrum: wartime inflation had doubled the price level, and yet the government remained committed to returning the pound to its pre-war parity of $4·86/£1. When inflation initially continued unabated—with prices rising by 40 per cent between 1918 and 1920—it became apparent that only a vigorous monetary restriction held any hope of a return to gold at the pre-war parity. When restriction was begun early in 1920, no contemporary economist was surprised to see the unemployment rate rise rapidly—from 4 per cent in 1920 to 17 per cent in 1921. In a world where few prices were perfectly flexible, a temporary rise in unemployment was the price that had to be paid if inflation was to be reversed.

Viewed in the light of subsequent experience, the striking feature of the 1920-21 recession was the extent to which the decline in aggregate demand manifested itself in deflation rather than in a drop in output. Real national income declined by 6 per cent, prices fell by 11 per cent and wages by 5 per cent. By 1922 real income had rebounded by 4 per cent, even as prices and wages declined by an additional 17 per cent. Over the next two years, prices and wages continued to decline, as real income continued its recovery; and unemployment, which had peaked at 17 per cent in 1921, had dropped by nearly 7 percentage points. By 1925, the level of prices had fallen to the point where, even though the pound remained somewhat over-valued, it was felt safe to restore full convertibility between gold and the pound. It is here that the real puzzle begins.

Interrupted only by the General Strike of 1926, real income rose strongly through the rest of the decade. Yet the unemployment rate remained lodged at around 10 per cent of the labour force. Moreover, although the price level continued to decline slowly, nominal wages remained constant. By 1929, even though both industrial production and real income exceeded their pre-war peaks, 10 per cent of the work-force—a million-man army of prime working age—remained unemployed.

Late in 1929, the monetary authorities in the United States began a policy of monetary restriction, hoping to quell growing speculation in the US stock market. The Federal Reserve raised the discount rate (the US equivalent of the bank rate) in 1929 and again in 1930, producing a precipitous decline in stock prices and a general rise in interest rates. The ensuing recession, and then depression, quickly enveloped the gold standard world—including Britain. Within a year, real income in Great Britain fell by 6 per cent, and by 1931 unemployment exceeded 20 per cent of the labour force. Despite the severity of the recession, nominal magnitudes were much less responsive than they had been only a

Chart 1:
UK Retail Price Index
(1913 = 100)

decade earlier: prices fell by only 5 per cent from 1930 to 1932 in Britain, while nominal wages declined by 3 per cent.

The on-going monetary contraction in the United States placed an intolerable strain on Britain's resolve to stay on the gold standard. Thus, in September of 1931—to the relief of most observers—the exchange rate of the pound was unpegged. Freed from externally imposed deflationary pressure, the British economy responded swiftly. Between 1932 and 1938 industrial production rose by more than 40 per cent, and real income surged upward at better than 5 per cent a year. As shown in Chart 1, prices fell slightly from 1932 to 1933, but then began moving upward at an accelerating rate, with inflation reaching 4 per cent per year by 1937. And while unemployment declined, as it had after the 1920-21 recession, *six years of economic expansion left the unemployment rate at a level more than three times its pre-war average.*

(b) The Historical Paradox

The historical paradox presented by the British economy in the inter-war period can best be appreciated by focussing on just two sets of numbers: real income and unemployment. During the half century preceding the First World War, real income in Britain grew at a rate of 2 per cent per year, while the unemployment rate averaged under 4 per cent. From 1920 to 1938—even accounting for the severe recessions of 1920-21 and 1930-31—real income continued to grow at a rate of 2 per cent per year, despite an unemployment rate that averaged *14 per cent.* To be sure, the growth of income during the inter-war period was erratic by historical standards: the two inter-war recessions, for example, were as severe as any experienced during the preceding 70 years. Yet the vigorous expansions of the late twenties and late thirties were sufficient to create a new England of modern suburbs, automobiles, and a general spread of prosperity unequalled in British history up until then.[1]

The vigorous growth in real income experienced in inter-war Britain stands in sharp contrast to the inter-war unemployment record. At peak levels (in the early thirties) there were over 2½ million working-age individuals registered as unemployed—some 22 per cent of the work-force. And even when unemployment was at its *lowest*—during the boom years of the late twenties and late thirties—at no time was the 'army of the unemployed' manned by fewer than one million people. Such figures were, as we have noted earlier, virtually without precedent in recorded British history. Indeed, when viewed solely from the perspective of the unemployment figures, the *best* of times during the inter-war period were on a par with the *worst* of times during the pre-war era.

The marked dissimilarity of the pictures presented by the real income figures on the one hand, and the unemployment numbers on the other, has struck other observers. As Glynn and Oxborrow (1976, p. 13) noted:

> 'The inter-war years present a paradox in British history. The popular image is of a period of depression with a gathering storm of fascism abroad. On the other hand, to set against that image is the record of economic growth. This record suggests that the inter-war years were a period of progress with rising material standards.'

All in all, the image is much like that which would be obtained if one viewed a photograph by placing the negative image firmly in

[1] Our characterisation of the growing prosperity of this era is hardly eccentric. Taylor (1965), in describing the period, entitles his page 301 'The New England'; and Pollard (1962) entitles one of his sub-chapters 'The Rise of the Standard of Living'.

front of the left eye and the positive image in front of the right eye.

Contemporary observers of the inter-war period were largely silent on this paradox, chiefly because they simply did not have the data that have since become available. Although attempts to calculate aggregate measures of national economic activity in Britain date back to the late 17th century, timely, accurate numbers are a luxury enjoyed only during the post-Second World War period.[1] Regular decennial and sporadic industrial censuses were, of course, available to inter-war observers, and gave them periodic snapshots of the state of the economy. There were also more regular indices of economic activity, such as those produced by the *Economist.* But the time-span between the nationwide censuses, combined with the absence of a generally accepted measure of economic activity, left inter-war observers with few means of directly inferring the annual, much less quarterly or monthly, performance of the economy.[2] In addition, while more detailed, authoritative, and frequent information on commodities subject to taxation and goods involved in international trade was available, such figures necessarily gave observers glimpses of the economy that were at best fragmentary.

Counting Numbers

There was, however, one item for which reliable, timely data were available: the number of persons unemployed (see Appendix, below, p. 37). As part of the process of paying unemployment benefits, the Ministry of Labour collected and published counts of the number of unemployed people on a *weekly* basis. And if one wished to know—in excruciating detail—the unemployment figures by region, by industry, by village, by sex or by age, one had only to wait for the monthly *Ministry of Labour Gazette* to

---

[1] See, for example, discussions contained in Mitchell and Deane (1962) and Feinstein (1972).

[2] This is not to demean the important work of Bowley (1937) and Clark (1932, 1937), among others. It is simply that national income accounting was in its infancy during the inter-war period and the data derived therefrom did not become an important factor in shaping views until after the Second World War. For example, Keynes (1930, pp. 86-88) [Vol. 2 of the *Treatise*] makes it clear that, as of 1930, there was no 'touchstone' series even for industrial production: he goes on for three pages trying to figure out which of the crude measures then available might be best.

arrive. In short, data on unemployment were far and away the most comprehensive and readily available measure of the economy's performance, and thus quickly came to dominate the opinions of inter-war observers and the actions of inter-war policy-makers.

To be sure, not everyone was equally entranced with the unemployment numbers, nor accepted them as gospel. Winston Churchill, for example, complained bitterly that

> 'Everyone who has some wonderful plan for enabling countries to get rich quickly, every advocate of the art of doing business at a loss—all point to these weekly totals exclaiming, "There! Up again this week. What did I tell you? We shall never be right until we adopt ——." The frequent general elections which so greatly hamper British trade revival are nearly all fought upon the numbers of the unemployed' (1930, p. 6).

And Edwin Cannan believed that the weekly and monthly unemployment figures so grossly distorted scholarly debate and public policy that publication of the figures should be stopped. Nevertheless, there is an old adage that 'any number is better than no number'. Given the ready availability of the Ministry of Labour figures, it is little wonder that inter-war observers and policy-makers focussed their attention and commentary on 'these weekly totals' of the unemployed.

The consequences of this focus on the unemployment rate are readily apparent in the most widely held inter-war views on the forces shaping Britain's economy. During the twenties many commentators—including Keynes—regarded Britain's attempt to return to gold at an over-valued rate, combined with the difficulties of wage deflation, as being the principal source of the high unemployment (Winch, 1969, Ch. 8). While this approach seems appealing for the early 1920s, it fails to explain why wages did not decline after 1923. From 1920 to 1923 wages fell by 30 per cent. From 1923 to 1929 nominal wages were constant, despite unemployment more than double the rate that had been consistent with pre-war price stability. Moreover, this approach cannot credibly appeal to the behaviour of unions as being the cause of inadequate wage deflation. Union membership was much higher in 1920-23 than in 1924-29. Indeed, membership declined from 6·3 million in 1920 to 3·4 million in 1929, a drop of

TABLE 1

UNEMPLOYMENT RATE AND OUTPUT GROWTH IN THE UK, 1924-38

Industry	Unemployment Rate %	Annual Output Growth %
Shipbuilding	37·4	-4·0
Coal-mining	21·6	-0·02
Textiles	18·4	1·3
Timber	13·0	5·1
Distributive trades	8·8	1·7
Gas, electricity, water	8·0	5·2
Electrical engineering	7·8	5·6

46 per cent.[1] The 'over-valued pound' explanation of high unemployment also fails on one additional point: the 'required' decline in wages could hardly have been a surprise to most people. The new exchange rate, reached in 1925, was widely regarded as the cornerstone, indeed, the *sine qua non*, of the government's economic policy.

Unemployment Due to Decline of Exports?

The heavy regional and industrial concentrations of unemployment during the inter-war years spawned yet another hypothesis. Generally, the highest unemployment rates were found in those industries that had traditionally specialised in exports—textiles, shipbuilding, the docks, and, after 1925, coal. Moreover, areas where these industries had been important—Wales, Northern England, and Scotland—suffered correspondingly higher-than-average rates of unemployment. Some sense of the disparity in unemployment rates may be gained with the aid of Table 1, which shows the unemployment rates for seven major industry groups for the period 1924-38, years for which this data is available at the industry level. The Table also shows the average growth in output for these industries over this period.

Industry-specific unemployment patterns such as these have

[1] Mitchell and Deane (1962), p. 69.

led to the hypothesis that the high national unemployment was importantly due to a decline in the demand for British exports (Clay, 1929a). For the early 1920s, the source of the depressed demand for exports was said to be Britain's attempts to return to gold at the pre-war parity. For the early 1930s, the causal mechanism was argued to be the world-wide decline in trade due to depression. The figures shown above certainly lend credence to the 'export hypothesis' of high national unemployment. After all, shipbuilding, coal-mining, and textiles were all important export industries, all experienced depressed conditions during the inter-war period, and all had high unemployment rates. Indeed, in Table 1, the simple correlation between unemployment rates and growth rates for these industries is -0·91: rapidly growing, prosperous industries tended to have low unemployment.

There are other troubling aspects of the depressed 'export hypothesis'. The most important declines in textile exports took place *during* the First World War, *not* the twenties. And while there were further reductions in textile exports in the thirties, this fails to explain the high unemployment rates in the cotton, woollen and linen industries during the twenties. Moreover, although inter-war coal exports were significantly below pre-war levels, coal production held up well during the inter-war years, save for 1921 and 1925—and in both years the decline in output was due to prolonged strikes. The experience of the docks in the inter-war period is perhaps the most troubling. From 1928 to 1931 the total work-force attached to this industry *rose*, even while the industry's unemployment rate averaged 34·3 per cent, rising from 31·7 per cent in 1928 to 39·2 per cent in 1931. During this same period, there were increasingly vigorous attempts, aided by the Ministry of Labour, to prevent new entry by workers seeking jobs in the docks (Royal Commission, 1932a, p. 89). If depressed exports were the principal cause of high unemployment, it is difficult to understand why workers were flocking to an industry where the rate of unemployment was 50 per cent higher than the national average.

Despite the appeal of the export hypothesis, it is equally clear that it cannot be the principal explanation of the high national unemployment during the period as a whole. For example, although the hypothesis is consistent with *reduced* employment in export industries, it fails to explain why workers remained *unemployed.* These industries had abnormally high unemployment rates *throughout* the inter-war years, even into the late thirties. After the First World War, returning soldiers and former munitions workers had found new employment without great difficulty; why should the transition from one peacetime employment to another have been so much more difficult?

It is tempting to argue that it was the difficulties of wage deflation that converted an export-led reduction in employment into elevated unemployment (*cf.* Winch, 1969). This argument has some appeal for understanding the high unemployment of the early twenties, but it fails to explain why wages did not decline during the second half of the decade. Union intransigence can hardly be argued to be the source of the sudden wage rigidity, since the importance of unions was *declining* during this period, not increasing. Moreover, it is difficult to argue that workers were somehow being systematically and chronically 'fooled' by government policy. Both the government's insistence on a return to gold at the pre-war parity, and the extent of deflation required to achieve that goal, were well known at the time. And to the extent that there were doubts among workers as to the government's resolve, these should have reflected themselves in less wage deflation during the first half of the 1920s, rather than during the second half. Our explanation (which follows that of Benjamin and Kochin (1979a)) for the failure of wages to continue falling is that the British economy was 'fully employed' at a 10 per cent or so unemployment rate, *given* the level of unemployment benefits.

Of course, if this explanation is correct, then it should be possible to explain variations in the unemployment rate across industries and regions in terms of unemployment benefits relative to wages paid in different industries or regions. In doing so, however, one must recognise the importance of the *source* of cross-sectional differences in wages. It is perhaps most natural to think of differences in wages across workers as arising from differences in the *productivity* of those workers—differences due to experience, training, or education. In fact, if wage differences are due to differences in productive abilities, then less productive (i.e., low-wage) people will find any given level of unemployment benefits relatively more attractive, and observed wages and unemployment rates will be negatively correlated: high-wage industries and regions will have low unemployment rates, while the converse will be true for low-wage sectors.

'Compensating Wage Differentials'

Occupations differ, however, as to on-the-job hazards, aesthetic features, and general working conditions. These differences in job conditions yield what are know as *compensating wage differentials*—that is, wage differentials that compensate workers for differences in working conditions (see Rosen, 1979, and Roback, 1982). At the margin, these differentials will just offset the pleasant or unpleasant characteristics of different jobs. For example, during the inter-war years, the observed wages of below-ground workers at coal mines exceeded the wages of above-ground workers by more than 60 per cent. Most or all of this difference was presumably due to the greater risks of working below ground, so that the 'true' wages (net of the compensating differentials) above and below ground were roughly equal. To the extent that job characteristics are responsible for differences in observed wages, then the correlation between observed wages and unemployment will be approximately *zero*, because true wages do not vary. In the case of the coal-mining example, it appears that wages are relatively high for below-ground miners, and that unemployment should be low among this group because benefits are low relative to wages. In fact, 'true' wages for below-ground miners are no higher than are wages for above-ground workers, implying that benefits are no less attractive.[1]

Both observed wages and observed unemployment rates also differ across industries (and thus regions, to the extent that industries tend to be geographically concentrated) because

[1] There is another reason that the observed variation between wages and unemployment may be zero. If wages are sufficiently high relative to benefits that even 'low-wage' workers find the benefits relatively unattractive, then there will be no observed cross-sectional variation in unemployment due to variation in wages. This, of course, would be expected to be observed in the immediate post-Second World War period, but also shows up in Eichengreen's (1987a) study of unemployment in inter-war London—for wages in London were by far the highest throughout Britain.

productive activity in some industries is inherently less stable than in others, often due to weather conditions. The classic example is the construction industry, where good weather leads to long work days and work weeks, while inclement weather can result in no activity at all. It is clear that when production varies over time, so will the employment of inputs. For labour, this implies variation in both the number of hours worked per person, and in the number of persons working. Since an 80-hour week is *not* counted in the official statistics as two weeks of employment, while a zero-hour week is counted as a week of unemployment, such industries have high measured unemployment rates; they are 'unemployment-intensive' industries. It is also true that measured wages in such industries tend to be high. In part, these high measured wages are spurious, because reported wage series often impute wages during employment to periods of unemployment to produce 'full-time equivalent' wages (*cf.* Chapman and Knight, 1953). In part, of course, the high measured wages are real, because workers are being compensated to perform 'inventory' services (i.e., to be ready for work whenever they are called). Whether real or spurious, however, measured wages will tend to be high in these unemployment-intensive industries, and thus the observed cross-sectional correlation between wages and unemployment will be *positive.*

Effects of Unemployment Insurance

Despite these *caveats*, there is evidence in the inter-war data that observed variations in unemployment across industries and regions can be explained, in part, by the generosity of unemployment insurance relative to wages. Given the nationwide uniformity of benefits by age-group and sex, high-wage workers should find any given level of benefits relatively unattractive as an alternative to work. Thus, to the extent that wages vary importantly due to differences in productivity, wage-rates and unemployment should be negatively correlated cross-sectionally. Benjamin and Kochin (1979a, 1982) have found three independent pieces of evidence that this was the case. First, the Unemployment Insurance Statutory Committee reported selected data on regional wages and unemployment for 1937. The correlation between regional wages and regional unemployment was –0·40. Second, a special nationwide survey of wages in 1938 revealed a similar pattern across industries. Among men, the correlation between wages and unemployment across industries was -0·30; among women the correlation was -0·54. Third, when the ratio of benefits to wages is used as an explanatory variable in explaining unemployment rates for the industries listed in Table 1 above, Benjamin and Kochin (1982) find that higher benefits relative to wages imply higher unemployment rates, results that 'are strikingly consistent with the notion that the insurance system had important effects during this period' (Benjamin and Kochin, 1982, p. 419).

At any rate, by the middle of the 1930s, hypotheses of the depressed exports type had become suspect. After 1929 interest rates declined, suggesting to many that monetary stringency could not be responsible for the high and rising unemployment that ensued (Friedman, 1967). Moreover, after the pound was floated in 1931, it became increasingly difficult to blame incorrect exchange rates for the lingering, chronic unemployment that plagued the 1930s. In response to these facts, Keynes began developing a new theory which could, he believed, explain prolonged high unemployment as an equilibrium phenomenon. To Keynes—and soon to most of the economics profession—the source of the problem was deficient aggregate demand; the remedy was deficit spending by the government.

Keynes's thesis is an appealing explanation for the sharp increases in unemployment in 1920 and 1930-31, which were mostly the result of monetary and other shocks to aggregate demand; moreover, adjustments to these shocks were undoubtedly hampered by the general contraction of international trade in the inter-war years. Nevertheless, any attempt to apply Keynes's reasoning to the prolonged unemployment that persisted through the late twenties and late thirties fails in the harsh glare of reality. Between 1920 and 1929, industrial production rose at an annual rate of 2·8 per cent while real income rose at the rate of 1·6 per cent per year. The corresponding increases per year for the period 1930-38 are 3·5 and 2·1 per cent. The implied annual growth rates between 1855 and 1913 are 2·3 and 1·9 per cent respectively. The above-average industrial expansion and real income growth of the late twenties and late thirties are simply inconsistent with the notion of deficient aggregate demand during these years. If we are to understand the army of the unemployed standing watch at the publication of *The General Theory*, we shall have to look elsewhere.

(c) Conclusions

Several salient features of the inter-war British economy emerge from the preceding discussion. *First*, despite the havoc wreaked by two of the most severe recessions in British history, the inter-war years constitute a period of vigorous economic growth. Industrial production in 1938 was more than 60 per cent above its level in 1920 and almost double its immediate pre-war level; moreover, real income grew at a rate identical to that experienced during the 60 years prior to the First World War.

Second, despite sustained economic expansion, unemployment rose to and remained at levels unprecedented in British history. The unemployment rate averaged three times the average rate observed during pre-war years, and even at its *lowest* it was as high as it had ever been prior to the war.

Third, the patterns of the major real economic variables during each of the two inter-war decades were remarkably similar. Real income and industrial production dropped sharply in 1920-21 and 1930-32, and then rebounded strongly; the unemployment rate mirrored these figures by rising sharply during recessions of the period and declining during the years of expansion.

Our examination of the inter-war British economy has left us with three puzzles. First, prices and wages were much more flexible in the early twenties than in the early thirties, dropping by 30 per cent in the first recession, but by less than 10 per cent in the second. Why was there a reduction in price and wage flexibility? Second, although the cyclical pattern of the unemployment rate was the same in the two decades, the thirties started with an unemployment rate that was six percentage points higher than at the beginning of the twenties. Why was the rate so much higher at the beginning of the thirties than at the start of the twenties? Finally, the extraordinarily high unemployment rates of the inter-war years were, on their face, inconsistent with the rapid economic growth of the period. Why did we observe high unemployment in the midst of growing prosperity? Before trying to resolve these puzzles fully, we must examine the American experience of the period. For illustration, the growth rates of real GNP are presented both for the USA and the UK in Chart 2.

Chart 2:
Real GNP Growth: USA and UK, 1920-38
(per cent per annum)

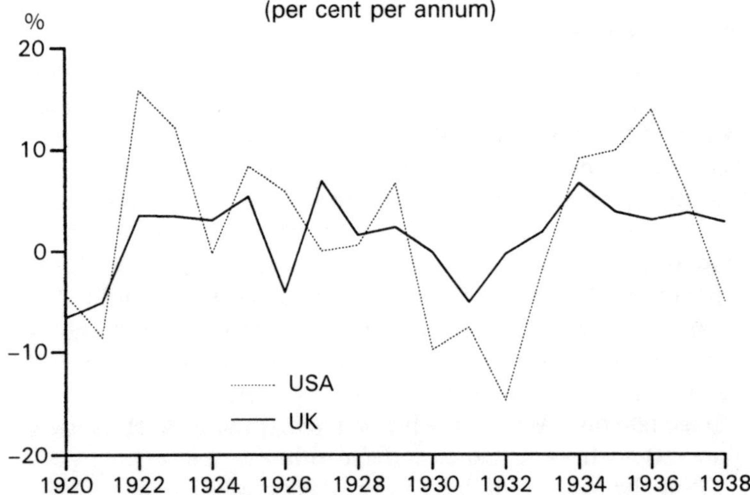

2. America Between the Wars

(a) The Historical Record

Although the United States remained a non-belligerent until April 1917, the American economy behaved during the First World War much like the British economy. The high demand for wartime materials produced large flows of gold into the United States. Accommodating monetary authorities permitted this inflow to be translated into rapid growth in the money supply, which in turn stimulated economic expansion and inflation.[1] America's entry into the war hastened this process, so that by 1918, real income was 20 per cent above its pre-war level and prices 70 per cent higher. After the War, US monetary authorities

[1] Until shortly before the First World War, the sole monetary authority in the USA was the US Treasury. In 1913 the Federal Reserve System was founded with some expectation that it would assume a rôle much like that of the Bank of England. During the War, the Treasury and the Federal Reserve System co-ordinated their efforts, with the Treasury acting as the senior partner. Late in 1919 the Federal Reserve System asserted itself as the leading player in the conduct of monetary policy, a rôle that has continued—except for the mid-thirties and the years during and immediately after the Second World War—ever since.

initially continued the monetary expansion; within just over a year, prices rose an additional 25 per cent.

Late in 1919 the Federal Reserve System, hoping to stem the inflation and facilitate a return to the Gold Standard, began a sharp monetary restriction. In a series of three steps beginning in November of that year, the Fed (as the System is commonly known) raised the discount rate to 7 per cent, from its wartime level of 4 per cent. The monetary stringency brought a swift response from the economy: real income dropped by nearly 15 per cent and prices declined by almost 40 per cent; the unemployment rate, which had been only 1·4 per cent in 1919, rose to 11·7 per cent in 1921.

Early in 1921 the Fed reversed its policy, and the money supply, which had fallen by more than 5 per cent, began to rise again. Real income rebounded quickly from the 1920-21 recession and, facilitated by stable, moderate monetary growth, grew steadily through the rest of the decade. Indeed, real income growth averaged 3·3 per cent per year from 1919 to 1929, a rate slightly higher than the 20th-century average of 3 per cent in the United States. The price level declined until 1922, but thereafter remained effectively constant through to the end of the decade. The unemployment rate also quickly shed the effects of the recession, and from 1922 to 1929 averaged 3·7 per cent—an average lower than that of any other period of comparable length in US history, save for the war-dominated 1940s.

The 1929 Stock Market Crash

The growing prosperity across the nation engendered rising confidence in the future—a confidence that manifested itself in sharply rising land and stock market prices in the late 1920s. In an effort to halt what it perceived to be speculative trading on the stock market, the Fed moved in 1929 to restrict banks' access to funds that were to be used for what the Fed viewed as speculative purposes. Banks found themselves unable to accommodate the credit demands of their customers and a wave of selling, culminating in the stock market crash of October 1929, produced sharply higher interest rates and a reduction in aggregate demand. Recession followed shortly thereafter, with real income and prices declining, and unemployment rising. By late 1930, a number of banks, including one prominent New York institution with the unfortunate name 'Bank of the United States', found themselves unable to meet the withdrawal demands of their customers. Despite having been founded chiefly to serve as a 'lender of last resort' for illiquid banks, the Fed refused to perform this function, thus precipitating a series of bank failures and a sharp drop in the public's confidence in the banking system. This in turn produced a series of bank runs, which in turn caused even more banks to fail. Between October 1930 and July 1931, nearly 1,400 banks holding 2 per cent of all commercial bank deposits failed, the money supply fell by 6 per cent (in addition to the 3 per cent it had fallen by October), and the decline in prices and output and increase in unemployment accelerated. By mid-year, both real income and the price level had fallen by 15 per cent and the unemployment rate stood at 16 per cent.

In September 1931 Britain left the Gold Standard and the Fed, fearing a loss of gold reserves, increased the discount rate sharply. This prompted a new series of bank failures and a massive conversion of deposits into currency, as commercial bank depositors sought safety for their funds. The money supply again dropped sharply as real income and prices fell by an additional 10 per cent, and unemployment climbed past 20 per cent. In the middle of 1932 the Fed finally (after an additional 1,800 banks had failed) began a modest injection of reserves into the system. When the injection was stopped later in the year, a new wave of bank failures began, producing an intensified conversion of deposits into currency and a further decline in the money supply. By the Spring of 1933, when the newly-inaugurated President Franklin Roosevelt declared a week-long, nationwide Banking Holiday, the carnage was complete: since 1929, more than 5,000 banks had failed, the money supply had fallen by more than a third, real income had dropped by 30 per cent, prices had declined by 40 per cent, and the unemployment rate stood at 25 per cent of the work-force.

Effects of Freeing the Dollar from Gold

For the next three-and-a-half years the Fed followed a policy of almost complete inactivity, perhaps chastened by its experience of the preceding four years, or possibly because a changing intellectual climate assigned priority to fiscal policy. Until late

1936, the only significant 'monetary policy' was undertaken by the Treasury. In 1933, as part of a series of steps designed to get the economy out of the Great Depression, Roosevelt unpegged the dollar from gold and allowed the dollar to devalue. This process culminated in January of 1934 with the establishment of an official gold price of $35 per ounce, nearly 75 per cent above its previous official level of $20·67.[1] Although the Treasury could have 'sterilised' the resulting inflow of gold from abroad by issuing bonds, it chose instead to pay for the gold by printing fiat money.[2] The consequence was that the monetary base—and thus the money supply—began rising rapidly. Between the beginning of 1933 and the end of 1936, the monetary base rose by 60 per cent and the money stock by 50 per cent.

The economy responded to this monetary stimulus with vigour. From 1933 to 1934, real income rose by 8·7 per cent. Over the next year it rose by 9·4 per cent, and from 1935 to 1936 the increase was 13 per cent—better than four times the long-run average growth rate in the United States. Indeed, by the end of 1936, real income had very nearly reached the level it had been in 1929. The unemployment rate declined sharply during this period as well, falling to 16·9 per cent in 1936 from its peak of 24·9 per cent in 1933. Employment, however, was less responsive to the monetary stimulus: total employment in 1936 was 44·4 million workers, more than a million fewer than had been employed in 1929.

The behaviour of the price level from 1933 to 1936 was erratic. Prices initially rose sharply, due to the operation of two forces. First, the *de facto* devaluation of the dollar in 1933 pushed up the prices of imported goods. Second, the National Industrial Recovery Act (NIRA), passed in the same year, pushed prices up by facilitating cartelisation among American businesses. The price of the dollar was stabilised in January 1934 and the NIRA was declared unconstitutional shortly thereafter. With these upward pressures on prices removed, the price level remained

---

[1] There was, of course, a catch: Americans were required to redeem their monetary holdings of gold—at the old price of $20·65 per ounce. Not surprisingly, many Americans suddenly decided to become numismatists.

[2] See Friedman and Schwartz (1963), pp. 299-419, for an extended discussion of this episode.

roughly constant through 1934, 1935 and the first half of 1936. During the second half of 1936 wholesale prices moved up noticeably, producing fear at the Federal Reserve of a sustained inflationary period.

Banks that survived the numerous banking panics of 1930-33 had decided that should bank runs ever begin anew, they would be prepared with adequate reserves to meet the withdrawal demands of their customers. Hence, between 1933 and 1936, banks had built their reserves up to a point at which they were double the legally required minimum. The Fed viewed these reserves in excess of the required minimum as being truly 'excess'—that is, as serving no economic function. The Fed also feared that improving economic conditions would stimulate a wave of new borrowing by businesses, which in turn would cause inflation to accelerate. To avoid having these excess reserves converted into new loans, the Fed doubled reserve requirements in a series of three steps in late 1936 and early 1937. This move, which converted the excess reserves into legally required reserves, left banks with no funds to meet contingencies. This in turn induced the banking system to sell securities and reduce loan portfolios so as to rebuild its excess reserve position. Monetary growth decelerated sharply and then turned negative. Interest rates rose sharply, industrial production and real income declined, and unemployment turned upward, reaching 19 per cent. Although the incipient inflation had been nipped in the bud, the cost was one of the most severe—albeit short-lived—recessions in American history.[1]

A year after raising reserve requirements, the Fed reduced them to their previous levels, apparently in response to worsening business conditions. The banking system once again had the cushion of excess reserves it desired, and responded by increasing its purchases of government securities and expanding loan portfolios. Interest rates dropped, industrial production and real income resumed their growth, and the unemployment rate once again turned downward. By 1941, the demands of war-torn

[1] It would be inappropriate to attribute the recession of 1937-38 wholly to the Fed. The contraction in the money supply was exacerbated by the Treasury, which began sterilising inflows of gold in 1936, thereby reducing the rate of growth of the monetary base. The Treasury subsequently halted sterilisation procedures, a move that helped the economy recover from the recession.

TABLE 2

REAL GROWTH AND UNEMPLOYMENT IN INTER-WAR AMERICA

Period	Annual Real Growth %	Unemployment Rate %
1919-39	1·8	10·9
1919-29	3·3	4·4
1929-39	0·3	16·9

Source: US Bureau of the Census, *Historical Statistics of the United States, Colonial Times to the 1970s*, New York: Basic Books, 1976, pp. 135, 224.2.

European nations had helped propel real income in America to a level 30 per cent above its peak in 1929 and nearly double its low of 1933. Despite this, America entered the war that year with an unemployment rate of 10 per cent—roughly double the long-term average. Eight years after it had ended, the scars of the Great Depression were still in evidence.

(b) The Historical Paradox

The two decades of the inter-war period in America are typically portrayed as being fundamentally different—the first, a time of prosperity and hope; the second, a period of depression and despair. Examining the evidence on real income and the unemployment rate for the two decades certainly does nothing to dispel this popular portrayal. Table 2 shows, for the period 1919-39 and for the two sub-periods 1919-29 and 1929-39, the record on real income growth and the unemployment rate. The disparities are striking.

Perhaps just as interesting is the fact that, of the two sub-periods, it is only the second (1929-39) that is 'out of line' with American experience in the 20th century. For example, in no other decade of this century has the average unemployment rate been as high as *one-half* of the average unemployment rate from 1929 to 1939.[1] Similarly, in no other decade of this century has the annual growth rate been as low as 1·0 per cent, much less the

[1] For obvious reasons, this comparison excludes decades (such as 1930-40) which include a portion of the period 1929-39.

TABLE 3

ANNUAL REAL GROWTH AND UNEMPLOYMENT IN THE USA: SELECTED DECADES

Period	Annual Real Growth %	Unemployment Rate %
1903-13	3·7	4·8
1919-29	3·3	4·4
1950-60	3·2	4·6
1960-70	3·9	4·8

Source: US Bureau of the Census, *Historical Statistics of the United States, Colonial Times to the 1970s*, *op. cit.*, pp. 135, 224.

0·3 per cent experienced from 1929 to 1939.[1] In contrast, the decade from 1919 to 1929 looks very much like three other decades in this century, in terms of real growth and unemployment, as shown in Table 3. In all four decades, real growth was higher than the 20th-century average and unemployment lower. In this sense, there is nothing particularly remarkable about the first half of the inter-war period in America.

How Could the 1930s Disaster Have Happened?

The sharp contrast between the twenties and the thirties in America leads on to the inevitable question: How could a decade of such sustained prosperity been followed by a decade of such unmitigated disaster? Early explanations focussed on a variety of factors, including protectionist efforts to insulate America from foreign competition, autonomous declines in investment (and perhaps consumption), and disastrous crop failures. None of these turns out to be particularly convincing.

It is true that protectionist sentiments ran high in America in the late twenties and early thirties, particularly in the agricultural sector. Yet most of this sentiment had little practical legislative or regulatory impact. Even the centre-piece of its achievements, the Smoot-Hawley Act of 1930, affected such a small part of the American economy that to attribute the Great Depression to it

[1] See the preceding footnote. The decade with the lowest growth rate is 1944-54, with an annual real growth rate of 1·2 per cent.

would be akin to attributing the loss of a kingdom to the want of a nail. The precipitous decline in investment expenditures in the early thirties—net investment actually became *negative*—has more appeal, but founders on one important point: there is no plausible evidence that the decline in investment was somehow autonomous in nature, rather than simply an induced response to other deflationary forces.[1] Finally, while it is true that the US experienced several major crop failures in the thirties, far and away the most important of these came in the mid-thirties—after recovery from the Great Depression had begun.

Perhaps the most convincing explanation for the Great Depression, developed by Friedman and Schwartz (1963), attributes the episode to gross ineptitude on the part of the Federal Reserve System in its conduct of monetary policy. As sketched in some detail above (pp. 27-28), a combination of inaction and inappropriate action on the part of the Fed caused a massive reduction in the money supply and thus aggregate demand between 1929 and 1933. This in turn produced a 30 per cent reduction in real income and a rise in the unemployment rate from 3·2 to 24·9 per cent.

The ensuing recovery, interrupted by the recession of 1937-38, is slightly more problematic. It is tempting to attribute the initial rise in income from 1933 to 1936 to expansionary New Deal fiscal policy, which more than doubled federal purchases of goods and services over this period. However, although the *rate of growth* of federal expenditures was high by historical standards, the *level* was small compared to the size of the economy: in 1933, government spending on goods and services amounted to a mere 4 per cent of GNP, and even by 1936 was only 6 per cent of GNP. It seems difficult to attribute the 60 per cent rise in real income from its 1933 trough to its 1937 peak to a $2·9 billion increase in annual government spending, particularly since government purchases of goods and services moved in the opposite direction to changes in GNP from 1937 to 1939. A far more plausible

[1] It is tempting to argue that the decline in investment was caused by the stock market crash of 1929, but was autonomous with respect to the rest of the economy, and thus the proximate cause of the Great Depression. This, of course, simply moves the question back one step: Why did the present discounted value of expected profits (as reflected in stock prices) decline? See also Friedman and Becker (1957), pp. 64-75.

explanation for recovery lies in the government's 1933 decision to devalue the dollar which, combined with its monetisation of the resulting gold inflow, produced a 53 per cent increase in the money supply.

The recession of 1937-38 and the subsequent pre-war expansion also appear most easily understood by monetary developments: late in 1936 and early in 1937 the Fed doubled reserve requirements, while the Treasury began sterilising gold flows, both of which produced a reduction in the money supply and thus in real income; a year later, both policies were reversed, yielding a sharp upturn in the money supply and real income.

Money Supply Answers—And a Puzzle

While the gyrations in real income from 1933 to 1939 thus seem to be best understood as being primarily the result of monetary forces, there remains a puzzle, expressed succinctly by Friedman and Schwartz:

> '. . . the most notable feature of the recovery after 1933 was not its rapidity but its incompleteness. Throughout the revival, unemployment remained large. Even at its cyclical peak in 1937, seasonally adjusted unemployment was 5·9 million; by the trough thirteen months later, it had risen to 10·6 million out of a labour force of nearly 54 million.' (1963, p. 493)

The most obvious way to view the 'notable . . . incompleteness' of recovery in the labour market is in terms of the unemployment rate. In 1937, after nearly four years of vigorous recovery, the rate was still four times as high as it had been in 1929. Indeed, it was not until 1943, almost two years after the United States entered the Second World War, that the unemployment rate got back to its levels of 1929. Alternatively, one can express the puzzle in terms of *employment*: despite the fact that real output rose by 60 per cent from 1933 to early 1937, employment rose by only 20 per cent. And even two years later, in 1939, there were 1·2 million *fewer* people employed than there had been in 1929, despite the fact that (i) real output was higher in 1939, and (ii) there were 6·7 million *more* people in the labour force in 1939 than in 1929.

The enigma posed by the sluggish recovery of employment in the middle and late 1930s is compounded by the behaviour of

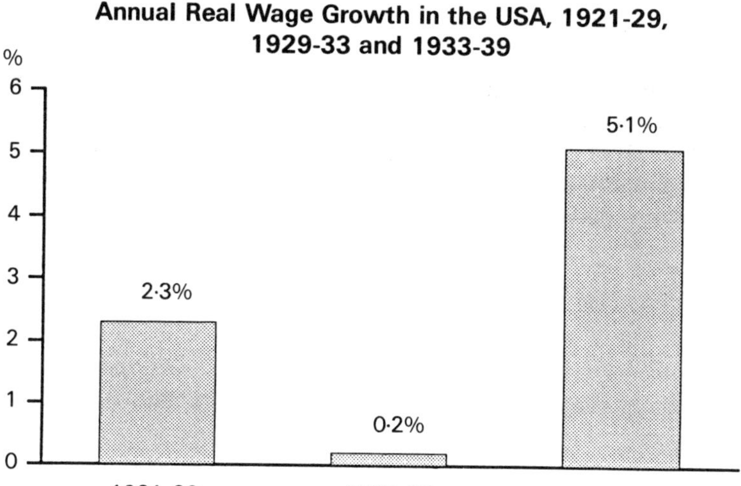

real wages. As shown in Chart 3, real wages in manufacturing had risen at an annual rate of 2·3 per cent per year from the cyclical trough in 1921 to the cyclical peak in 1929, a rate very close to the 20th-century average of about 2 per cent. During the Great Depression real wages first rose slightly and then declined almost as much, yielding an annual growth rate of only 0·2 per cent for the years 1929 to 1933. During the years from 1933 to 1939, however, real wages rose at an annual rate of 5·1 per cent—a rate more than *double* the long-run average, and sharply in contrast to the periods immediately prior to 1933. The combinations of extremely rapid real wage growth in the face of high residual unemployment in the middle and late thirties, and the concurrent sluggish employment growth in the midst of rapidly growing real output, remain the least well understood features of the inter-war period in the United States.

(c) Conclusions

We saw in our earlier discussion of Britain that the unemployment rate and the behaviour of real income during both decades of the inter-war period appear mutually inconsistent: growth was normal, unemployment was distinctly abnormal. For the United States, the puzzle is somewhat different: both unemployment and real growth appear normal in the twenties, while both appear distinctly abnormal in the thirties. Research over the last 30 years, spearheaded by the work of Friedman and Schwartz (1963), has solved much of the mystery of the behaviour of real income in the thirties. There remains, however, the puzzle of why the labour market responded as it did in the aftermath of the Great Depression. Before attempting to resolve this puzzle, some additional groundwork is required, and to this we now turn.

APPENDIX TO CHAPTER 2

Measuring Unemployment

The systems of measuring unemployment in inter-war Britain and America were markedly different. The British method of measurement was based on the unemployment insurance system; it was a literal head count of those individuals who were covered by the insurance scheme and who were unemployed. Until late in the inter-war period, America did not even have an unemployment insurance system, and even once it was founded, it covered only a small fraction of the work-force. The methodological basis for the American numbers (which were actually not even published for the first time until 1948) is a survey of a sample of individuals which inquires into their labour force and employment status.

Within each country, the reported unemployment series is fully comparable over time within the inter-war period. Thus, an unemployment rate in Britain of, say, 10·8 per cent in 1928 is comparable to the unemployment rate of 10·8 per cent in 1937. Considerably more care must be taken when comparing unemployment rates across countries during the inter-war period, and across time within a given country. Subject to the *caveats* noted below, the unemployment numbers for both countries can be used as rough guides when comparing (i) labour market conditions during the inter-war period *versus* conditions today; and (ii) inter-war labour market conditions in one country, *versus* conditions in the other country. Thus a 20 per cent unemployment rate in inter-war Britain clearly signified worse labour market conditions than, say, a 10 per cent unemployment rate in Britain today, or a 10 per cent unemployment rate in inter-war America. As the numbers which are being compared get closer together numerically, the substantive import of an arithmetic difference becomes questionable. Thus, whether an unemployment rate of, say, 10 per cent in inter-war Britain was 'really' different from an 8 per cent unemployment rate in either inter-war America or Britain today, may be almost unknowable. Readers wishing to undertake more detailed comparisons than those presented in the text should consult Benjamin and Kochin (1979a, 1982) and Darby (1976) for more details.

(i) Britain

The reported unemployment rate in inter-war Britain is a measure of unemployment among persons covered by the unemployment insurance system, a group that comprised about 70 per cent of the total work-force. (For all practical purposes, excluding agricultural and domestic workers, all privately employed manual workers over the age of 16 were covered by unemployment insurance during the inter-war series. Non-manual workers such as civil servants and teachers were not added to the insurance system until 1948, and since such workers tend to have lower-than-average unemployment rates, their addition to the system tended to lower measured unemployment rates in post-war Britain relative to inter-war Britain. See Benjamin and Kochin (1982) for more details.)

The unit of counting was the 'lodged' unemployment book, a two-page card in which was kept a record of each worker's insurance contributions and benefits. When an insured person became unemployed, he was to obtain his employment book from his employer and 'lodge' it with the employment exchange, where it remained for the duration of his unemployment. Upon obtaining work the individual had to retrieve his book from the exchange and give it to his employer, who affixed contribution stamps therein for each week of employment.

Unemployment books expired in July of each year, at which point they were delivered to the employment exchange to be exchanged for new ones. The denominator of the unemployment rate is the number of books issued in July of the corresponding calendar year. The annual unemployment rate is the average number of persons unemployed in each month divided by the number of books issued in July. People employed on government public works or relief projects were counted as being employed. People attending government training centres were counted as unemployed; at no time did the number of such people exceed 10,000 during the inter-war period. A convenient series on the unemployment rate is available in the Department of Employment and Productivity's *British Labour Statistics* (1971).

With the exception of the census of 1931, the insurance system provides the only comprehensive, original source series on unemployment in inter-war Britain. And with the exception of trade union returns for the years 1920-26, the insurance system also provides the only original source time-series on unemployment in inter-war Britain. Feinstein (1972) presents a series that purports to be an economy-wide (including industries not covered by the insurance system) time-series on unemployment in inter-war Britain. His method of construction, however, implicitly assumes that incentives facing people covered by unemployment insurance were identical to those *not* covered by insurance—which of course begs the entire question of the incentive effects of the insurance system.

Although the unemployment insurance numbers are by far the most useful unemployment figures for the inter-war years, some caution must be exercised in interpreting them. The inter-war insurance system excluded from coverage many non-manual workers. Such workers tend to have inherently lower unemployment rates than do manual workers.[1] Thus, even if the insurance system had no effects on the unemployment rates of covered workers, the fact that it only covered workers who tended to have higher-than-average unemployment rates means that the inter-war insurance unemployment rates tended to overstate the overall economy-wide unemployment rate of the time.

Immediately after the Second World War, the insurance system was expanded to cover these non-manual workers. This change in coverage alone tended to lower the measured unemployment rate, because it brought into the system many workers with inherently low unemployment rates. This change in coverage means that comparisons between inter-war and post-war unemployment rates should be made only with great circumspection (*cf.* Benjamin and Kochin (1982) for a fuller discussion).

There were two other changes in the post-war years that also suggest that the post-war unemployment figures are abnormally low relative to previous periods in British history (including the years before the First World War). First there is the matter of 'short-time' working arrangements, commonplace even before the First World War. As discussed in detail in Chapter 3, the

[1] This is partly because of the occupations of non-manual workers (e.g., managers), and partly because of the industries in which they work (e.g., the Civil Service).

administrative rules of the inter-war insurance system fostered the proliferation of short-time working arrangements. During the inter-war years it was common for workers to form 'pools' with five or six members. The members arranged with their employer systematically to have one or two in each pool 'play off' (be temporarily laid off) in turn, enabling them to retain continuous eligibility for benefits. The practice of organised short-time work such as this was sufficiently common that it quickly became known as the 'OXO' system, due to the frequently observed arrangement of alternating days of work (O) and unemployment (X).

In a series of administrative decisions beginning early in the post-war period, the OXO system of long-term alternating work and benefit receipt has been made illegal in Britain (Calvert, 1974). Since OXO systems were the single most important way in which the insurance system was exploited in the inter-war period, its post-war elimination means that post-war unemployment rates are lower than would otherwise be the case.

Second, there is the matter of the widespread post-war use of 'guaranteed work' contracts, which were effectively unknown before the Second World War (Benjamin and Kochin, 1982). Such contracts provide that workers who are laid off are paid a proportion of their normal pay. In return the workers must stand ready to work when recalled. When they are being paid they are ineligible for unemployment benefits, and when they are subject to recall they cannot sign the unemployment registers.

The spread of guaranteed work contracts has fundamentally altered the meaning of post-war unemployment figures. Jobs in industries that had always been seasonal industries, such as coal-mining, have become year-round positions. In the textile industry, and at the docks, where casual, piece-rate work accompanied by frequent lay-offs had always been the norm, workers have effectively become permanent workers under guaranteed-work contracts. Moreover, these workers (as well as workers in other industries) never even show up in the post-war unemployment statistics when they are laid off. Thus, the spread of guaranteed-work contracts makes the reported unemployment rates of the post-war period unlike those of any other period in British history.

(ii) America

A comprehensive unemployment rate for inter-war America was not produced until after the Second World War (see Lebergott, 1948). The methods used to construct the inter-war data represent an attempt to approximate, *ex post*, the current survey methods used by the Bureau of Labor Statistics (BLS). Currently, the BLS interviews approximately 60,000 households each month to determine the work activity of each household member aged 16 and over during the survey week. Such a person is counted as being employed if he (i) worked one hour or more as a paid employee, (ii) worked 15 hours or more without pay in a family enterprise, or (iii) held a job from which that person was temporarily absent. All those not satisfying these criteria fall into one of two other groups. To be considered *unemployed*, a person must be (i) available for work, and (ii) have made specific efforts to find work during the preceding four weeks. People who are not employed and neither looking for nor available for work are considered to be *out of the labour force.* The labour force is the total of the number of people employed and unemployed, while the unemployment rate is simply the number of people unemployed divided by the labour force.

The central point at issue concerning the inter-war unemployment rates for America is the treatment of individuals active in the emergency relief programmes of the period. According to the US Bureau of the Census (1947):

> 'During the period in which public emergency work projects were being conducted by the Works Project Administration (WPA), the National Youth Administration (NYA), the Civilian Conservation Corps (CCC) and State and local work relief agencies . . ., persons at work on, or assigned to, such projects were also included among the unemployed.' (p. 1)

This methodology was followed by Lebergott and the BLS in constructing the estimates of unemployment and unemployment rates for America during the inter-war period (see Darby, 1976).

During the years 1930-31 and early 1932, the number of people affected by this counting method was modest. By 1933, nearly 500,000 people were involved, and from 1934 to 1940, there were up to 3½ million people thus engaged but counted as unemployed following this convention. Darby (1976) simply asserts that these individuals should be counted exactly as if they had been gainfully employed in the private sector or on any other government job (such as delivering the mail). In Chapter 5 we attempt to determine how many of these individuals would in practice have obtained such employment had the emergency work programmes been curtailed.

3

LOVE ON THE DOLE

Introduction

IN THE PREVIOUS CHAPTERS we have enumerated a number of puzzles that characterised the inter-war period in Great Britain and the United States. Here we lay the groundwork for solving these puzzles. Our solution—spelled out in detail in the chapters that follow—rests on one simple proposition: *lowering the cost of any activity will induce people to engage in more of that activity.* This proposition, which economists call the Law of Demand, is the single most powerful and well-established proposition in all of economics—and perhaps in all of the social sciences. To take a few commonplace observations, the Law of Demand explains why buildings are taller in central areas of major cities than in outlying suburbs; why fresh fruits and vegetables are less expensive when they are in season; and why many people willingly buy balcony seats, even though most would agree that orchestra seats are superior.[1]

In the present instance, the relevant application of the Law of Demand relates to unemployment: *if the cost of being unemployed is lowered, more people will choose to be unemployed.*

[1] Land is less expensive in the suburbs so people consume more of it, by building 'out' rather than 'up'; when fruits and vegetables are in season, individuals are induced to consume the additional supplies only because the prices are lower; similarly, people choose 'inferior' balcony seats rather than 'superior' orchestra seats not because they are ignorant, but because the price of balcony seats is lower.

One way to lower the cost of unemployment is to pay people to become unemployed, through some form of unemployment compensation scheme. We argue here that this is exactly what happened in inter-war Britain, and during the last third of the inter-war period in America: the respective governments of the two nations introduced and expanded schemes of unemployment compensation (called 'insurance' in Britain and 'relief' in America) that reduced the cost of being unemployed. As a result, more people willingly chose to become unemployed. And, we contend, once the effects of these unemployment compensation schemes are accounted for, the remaining puzzles of high inter-war unemployment are eliminated.

At the outset it is essential to understand what the Law of Demand does not assert. It does not, for example, imply that *all* buildings in the centre of cities will be skyscrapers, nor that skyscrapers will *never* be observed in the suburbs; instead it predicts that the *average height* of buildings will be greater in city centres than in the suburbs. Similarly, the Law of Demand does not imply that fresh fruits and vegetables will be inexpensive (in some absolute sense) while in season, nor that everyone will eat only produce that is in season; rather, it implies that the price of fresh produce in season will be lower than it is out of season, and that *more* people will eat *more* fresh produce in season than out of season. Moreover, the Law of Demand does not assert that everyone will forgo orchestra seats when balcony seats are cheaper, only that *more* people will choose to do so. Finally, and most importantly, the Law of Demand does *not* predict that unemployment compensation schemes will induce everyone to become unemployed, nor does it imply that persons becoming unemployed will necessarily do so permanently. Instead it predicts that *some* additional people will choose unemployment if they are paid to do so, and that they will choose *more* of it.

Our primary goal in this chapter is to lay out the historical evolution and broad institutional features of the unemployment compensation schemes adopted in inter-war Britain and America. We do not pretend to be either encyclopaedic or exhaustive. We seek instead to present the essential details required to understand how an act as simple as lowering the cost of an activity can fundamentally alter the course of economic history and mould the views of observers into shapes that have not disappeared 60 years later.

1. Unemployment Insurance in Inter-War Britain

(a) The Essentials

Until shortly before the First World War there was no centrally financed or administered unemployment insurance in Britain. Public assistance for unemployed persons was limited to locally administered and financed poor relief. The receipt of Poor Law benefits was tied to poverty rather than to unemployment, and the provisions for receipt were burdensome. Indeed, these provisions were sufficiently onerous that even beggars used as a clincher in their pleas that if alms were not given they would be 'pauperised'—that is, forced to accept poor relief. Save for individual acts of charity, the only assistance available to unemployed people who were not yet destitute were privately funded unemployment assistance funds operated by a few trade unions.

In 1908, after an exhaustive and critical review of existing conditions, the Poor Law Commission recommended a series of social reforms. The Liberal Government took many of these recommendations to heart, establishing old-age pensions, medical insurance and the employment exchanges—thereby erecting the foundations of the modern welfare state in Britain. For our purposes, the key element in this legislative package was the Unemployment Insurance Act of 1911, which made centrally administered unemployment insurance available to about 15 per cent of the work-force. In many respects, the Act was patterned after the unemployment assistance funds operated by some unions. Thus, a worker who had a steady employment record could, upon retirement, receive a lump-sum distribution of any of his insurance contributions that had not been paid him in unemployment benefits. This provision introduced an element of 'experience rating' to the system, for it made it clear to workers that the choice of collecting current benefits came at the expense of a reduction in any future refunds. The Act was also intended to be actuarially sound, accumulating reserves in good times so that payments could be made in bad times. This intention met with initial success: by the end of the First World War, contributions exceeded benefit payments by a factor of more than five to one. Subsequent events, most notably the high unemployment of the twenties, ultimately exhausted the fund, leading to heavy subsidisation out of the general revenues of the Exchequer throughout most of the inter-war period.[1]

Amendments to the Act in 1916 and 1919 extended benefits to an additional 10 per cent of the work-force and increased nominal benefits, although they did not change the fundamental insurance-based design of the system. Moreover, the high inflation during and immediately after the First World War significantly eroded real benefits; in conjunction with the buoyant state of aggregate demand, this effect made the receipt of unemployment benefits a relatively unattractive alternative to work for most individuals.

1920 Liberalisation of the System

The unemployment insurance system that emerged from the First World War was fundamentally altered by the Unemployment Insurance Act of 1920, which removed many of the system's safeguards and increased benefits by nearly 40 per cent. The Act also extended coverage to more than 11 million workers; with the exception of agricultural and domestic workers, virtually all privately employed wage-earners over the age of 16 were thus included. The sea change begun in 1920 was amplified in the decade to follow. Contributory requirements that workers had to satisfy to become eligible for benefits were successively relaxed; weekly insurance benefits were raised, even in the face of a declining price level; and workers became eligible to receive benefits for increasingly extended periods. This liberalisation of the system put it under great financial strain and led to ever more funding out of the general revenues of the Exchequer. The strain also led to attempts by the government partially to offset the growing allure of unemployment benefits by, for example, requiring that benefit claimants be 'genuinely seeking work'.

Nevertheless, the net effect was a progressive liberalisation of the system during the twenties that made the dole an increasingly attractive alternative to work: by 1931, weekly benefits exceeded 50 per cent of average weekly wages, and an unemployed adult who had made 30 weekly insurance contributions at *any* time in his working career could draw full insurance benefits for an *unlimited* period.[2]

---

[1] See Douglas and Director (1931), pp. 401-27.

[2] Cf. Benjamin and Kochin (1979a, 1982), and Deacon (1976).

By 1931, the munificence of the system, combined with an unemployment rate that had not been appreciably below 10 per cent since 1920, had imposed heavy financial losses on the insurance fund. Therefore, as part of a comprehensive economy move originally aimed at saving the gold rate of the pound, the government moved to reduce both the generosity and scope of the system. The Unemployment Insurance (National Economy) Orders of October 1931 cut basic weekly benefits by 10 per cent, stiffened contributory requirements, and limited the maximum duration for receipt of benefits to 26 weeks in any insurance year. These measures were kept in place until 1934, when benefits were restored to their previous levels, and the requirements for the receipt of benefits were relaxed. Benefits were increased again in 1936 and 1938, so that on the eve of Britain's entry into the Second World War, insured workers were indefinitely eligible to receive benefits equal to nearly 60 per cent of average wages. *The generosity of the unemployment insurance system had reduced the cost of being unemployed in Britain to a level never before observed.*

(b) Some Unusual Features

More remarkable than the generosity of the inter-war unemployment insurance system were three administrative features that have received little attention but—as we shall see—were crucial in shaping its impact. First, the inter-war system had no 'experience rating', which is to say that the required insurance contributions (premiums) paid by worker and employer were unrelated to their past unemployment experience. As we noted earlier, the Act of 1911 had originally provided that each worker who collected less in unemployment benefits than he paid in contributions could collect the difference upon retirement. This provision was dropped after the First World War, so that a worker faced with a choice between accepting a wage cut or a lay-off no longer had an incentive to accept the wage cut to preserve his contributions fund. Similarly, employers paid no higher premiums if their work-force collected benefits due to unemployment, and paid no lower contributions if they kept their workers on the pay-roll at lower wages rather than laying them off. This lack of experience rating during the inter-war years made the receipt of unemployment benefits appear to be without cost to either employee or employer. Thus, in the event of a decline in demand, worker and employer had a joint incentive to adjust via lay-offs rather than wage cuts.

The Structure of Benefits

The second unusual administrative feature of the inter-war system involved the structure of benefits. Although benefits differed according to sex (higher for men) and age (rising as one moved from ages 16-17 to 18-20 to 21 and over), they were not otherwise tied to the wages of workers. As a result, a given statutory level of benefits was translated into wide variation in the ratio of benefits to wages, due to the variation in wages across workers. In general, such an arrangement will induce more unemployment than will a system in which benefits are proportional to wages, because low-wage workers will find the fixed benefits to be an extraordinarily attractive alternative to work.[1]

'Continuous' Unemployment

The third unusual aspect of the inter-war system was perhaps the most important. Throughout the period, benefits were payable for spells of unemployment as short as *one day*, provided that a waiting period subsequent to the onset of unemployment had been served. Under the Act of 1920, the waiting period was the first three days of a continuous period of unemployment, but this was increased to one week (i.e., six working days) in June 1921.[2] The peculiarity arose in the implementation of the waiting period: any three days of unemployment during any six consecutive working days were treated as 'continuous' unemployment. In addition, a pair of such three-day periods, occurring within three to 10 weeks of one another, could be 'linked up' to form a six-day period of continuous unemployment. Once the waiting period, thus defined, had been served, a further waiting period was not required unless the 'bridge' between two three-day periods of continuous unemployment had been broken. In

---

[1] See Benjamin and Kochin (1979a), p. 447, for a further discussion of this point.

[2] The waiting period remained at one week through the rest of our period, save for August 1924 to October 1925 and onwards from March 1937, when it was three days.

practice, therefore, with the exception of the first spell of unemployment of a worker's career, a modicum of judicious timing ensured him of eligibility for benefits beginning with the *first day* of any unemployment.[1]

This definition of 'continuous' unemployment fostered the widespread practice of 'short-time' working.[2] During the inter-war years it was common for workers to form 'pools' with five or six members. The members arranged with their employer systematically to have one or two in each pool 'play off' (be temporarily laid off) in turn, enabling them to retain continuous eligibility for benefits. The practice of organised short-time work such as this was sufficiently common that it quickly became known as the 'OXO' system, due to the frequently observed arrangement of alternating days of work (O) and unemployment (X). Workers participating in organised short-time plans could be held ineligible for benefits in any week in which their short-time earnings exceeded one-half of their full-time earnings. Thus the most commonly observed OXO arrangement involved three days each of work and unemployment per week—'three on the book and three on the hook'—for this met the earnings constraint whilst also satisfying the definition of continuous unemployment.[3]

Churchill and Beveridge on Unemployment Insurance

The role of the insurance system in encouraging the development of OXO schemes was not lost on inter-war observers. Winston Churchill, for example, complained that:

> 'British employers have lent themselves to an abuse of the system of unemployment insurance. . . . They systematically arrange to give their workers just that amount of employment that will enable them to qualify for the benefit.' (Churchill, 1930, p. 7)

Churchill's contention is graphically illustrated in a leaflet circulated by a colliery in connection with a labour dispute:

---

[1] See Royal Commission on Unemployment Insurance (1932a), pp. 223-24, and Burns (1941), pp. 102, 151.

[2] The practice of short-time had been observed before the First World War, but chiefly only in a few seasonal industries.

[3] *Cf. Unemployment Insurance in Great Britain* (1925), pp. 41, 53-54, 58; Gilson (1931), pp. 664-65; Royal Commission on Unemployment Insurance (1932a), pp. 98-102, (1932b), pp. 630-31.

> 'The pits will be so worked as to enable the employees to qualify for three days' unemployment in alternate weeks. The unemployment benefit will therefore more than cover the reduction in wages.' (Bakke, 1935, p. 62)

Even W. H. Beveridge, head of the London School of Economics at the time, and ever sympathetic to the plight of the unemployed, wrote that:

> '. . . industries such as cotton [textiles] which was practising short time as a temporary measure during trade depressions, is tending now to practice it continually and to keep an excessive labour force together at the cost of the unemployment fund' (Beveridge, 1930, p. 46).

Beveridge's wording is worth emphasising. First, he refers to the use of short-time work during trade depressions in the *past tense*, suggesting that depression was not the cause of short-time work arrangements during the late twenties. Second, he refers to prior short-time arrangements as 'temporary', suggesting that they were fundamentally different from the continuous nature of the OXO schemes of the inter-war period. Finally, it is clear that Beveridge regarded system-induced short-time work as producing a *net increase* in unemployment, for otherwise he would not have been concerned about the added cost to the unemployment fund of OXO schemes.

The importance of schemes like the OXO system in shaping both the level and the character of inter-war unemployment is clear in the Ministry of Labour's statistics. In any given week, unemployment due to short-time work routinely accounted for one-quarter to one-third of all unemployment. Moreover, in a one per cent sample of claimants to benefits (on 2 February 1931), the Royal Commission on Unemployment Insurance found that claimants had averaged 7·3 separate spells of unemployment during 1930. The median length of the spells was only four days. The popular portrayal of unemployment in inter-war Britain is that of continuous joblessness, grinding on year after year; figures such as these are much more suggestive of workers who were routinely choosing 'just that amount of employment that will enable them to qualify for the benefit'.

(c) Women and Children

Thus far we have treated the benefits and eligibility rules of the inter-war system as though they were uniform across all insured workers. In fact, there were differences across workers, the most important of which applied to younger workers and married women. Fully to appreciate the rôle of unemployment insurance in shaping behaviour during the inter-war period, these differences must be recognised.

(i) Juveniles

During the inter-war period the school-leaving age in Britain was 14, and only infrequently did individuals pursue their education for a substantial period thereafter. Surveys of insured workers reveal that between 90 and 95 per cent of them left school prior to age 15 and more than 95 per cent of them had obtained their first job by age 16—the age at which coverage by the insurance system began.[1] Insurance benefits available to single juveniles (aged less than 18) were extremely low, averaging only about 6·5 shillings (less than 15 per cent of average weekly wages). At age 18, weekly benefits more than doubled, and at age 21, there was a further rise of 50 per cent. Since the system paid additional benefits for both adult and minor dependants, the effective benefits facing claimants must have risen at an even faster rate as they passed through ages 16 to 21. Of course, wages would be expected to rise over this age-span due to growing work experience, and it is benefits *relative* to wages that are relevant for the choice between employment and unemployment. In fact, based on wage agreements reported regularly in the *Ministry of Labour Gazette*, wages rose less than half as fast as benefits over the age-span 16 to 21, implying substantial increases in benefits relative to wages at ages 18 and 21.

In addition to the relatively low statutory benefit rates for juveniles, it was impossible for many of them to collect *any* benefits. Before achieving initial eligibility for unemployment benefits, insured persons had to pay between 20 and 30 weekly contributions. Since insurance coverage did not begin until age

[1] *Cf. Ministry of Labour Gazette*, September 1932 and September 1933, and Royal Commission on Unemployment Insurance (1932b), pt. 5. After September 1934 coverage was extended to juveniles aged 14 and 15.

16, no contributions were paid until this age,[1] implying that juveniles spent much of their early years in the system ineligible for any benefits at all. In addition, with trivial exceptions, juveniles were ineligible for any of the supplementary benefits schemes designed to aid people unable to satisfy contributory requirements; thus there were substantial numbers of juveniles for whom the effective ratio of benefits to wages was zero.

Quite simply, then, the unemployment insurance system made unemployment relatively unattractive for juveniles: benefits were low relative to wages, and many juveniles were ineligible for any benefits at all. Interestingly enough, *juvenile unemployment was also very low during the inter-war period*—a point to which we return in Chapter 5.

(ii) Married Women

During the inter-war years it was customary in some lines of business and branches of local civil service to refuse to hire married women and to discharge women employees if they got married. Until 1931, women who thus became unemployed were eligible for unemployment benefits as soon as they had satisfied the standard waiting period, even if they (a) married knowing that their employer discharged married women, or (b) quit in anticipation of the application of such a policy.[2]

By 1930 it was widely argued that married women were exploiting this feature of the insurance system by collecting post-nuptial benefits even when they had no intention of returning to work. Thus, it was said, the system had become merely a convenient means of supplementing newly-weds' incomes as they set about starting a family. To alleviate this and other perceived irregularities in the system, the government issued the Anomalies Regulations in October 1931. As applied to married women, the regulations imposed substantially more demanding contribution requirements than required of other applicants for

[1] But see n. 1, above, p. 51.

[2] Gilson (1931), pp. 116, 314; Cohen (1938), p. 136; and Umpire's Decision 122 (4/3/21), reprinted in Unemployment Compensation Interpretation Service (1938). If a woman quit in the absence of such a policy, she was required to wait six weeks for benefits, the same period required for all other persons who voluntarily left their jobs.

benefits.[1] Exceptions to these added requirements were made only for women whose husbands were incapacitated from work or unemployed and not receiving benefits.

The Anomalies Regulations thus put newly married women in much the same position as juveniles: they had to 'begin anew' to establish their contributions records, rather than enjoying the much more lenient standards applicable to other people who were discharged. The more stringent contributory requirements of the Anomalies Regulations produced widespread disallowances of the benefits claims of married women. And, interestingly enough, the implementation of the Regulations was soon followed by a sharp drop in unemployment among married women and a decline in unemployment among women relative to unemployment among men—facts to which we shall return in Chapter 5.

(d) The Perspective of Inter-War Observers

Not surprisingly, the widespread nature of unemployment, combined with the ready availability of statistics detailing its extent, generated numerous attempts to explain it. As we noted earlier, most of these efforts were driven by a belief that the demand for labour was deficient. However, some observers—led by Jacques Rueff and Edwin Cannan—argued that the high unemployment was caused in large part by the high benefits and lenient administrative features of the unemployment insurance system.

Rueff on the Insurance System

Rueff's explanation was stimulated by the high positive correlation he observed between unemployment and real wages in inter-war Britain.[2] To him the unemployment insurance system acted much like a government price-support system. A key element in

---

[1] Married women had to have paid a minimum of 15 weekly contributions since marriage. In addition, if more than six months had elapsed since marriage, they had to have paid at least eight contributions during the six months preceding the beginning of the current benefit quarter (Ministry of Labour, 1933). See also Benjamin and Kochin (1979a), p. 462.

[2] The association between high real wages and high unemployment is shown graphically in Rueff (1925). Shortly thereafter, Sir Josiah Stamp applied the then new technique of correlation analysis to Rueff's data. As published in the *Financial Times*, Supplement (1926, p. vi), the correlation was 0·95 for 1919-25.

his argument was the rôle played by labour unions, for he believed that the high level of unemployment benefits encouraged the unions to resist reductions in nominal wages, regardless of the level of unemployment among their members:

> 'The discipline of the trade unions ... is extremely powerful in England and the system of collective bargaining more widely used than elsewhere. But this tradition would have been insufficient to maintain the resistance of the unemployed worker to the inevitable movements in wages if a policy of subsidising the unemployed which was both generous and paid for by the nation had not permitted the unemployed to remain indefinitely without work rather than violate union orders' (Rueff (1925), pp. 433-34, translated from the French and reported in Benjamin and Kochin (1979a), n. 42).

Rueff also argued that the insurance system acted directly on individuals, by making unemployment a superior alternative to employment available at wages little if any higher than unemployment benefits:

> 'The consequence of [the insurance system] was to set a minimum level of wages below which the worker preferred to tap the dole rather than work for a wage which could only give him a small excess over the sum which he could receive as unemployed. It seems clear that until the beginning of 1923 wages in England followed the decline in prices and would have reached an equilibrium level. They then brusquely stopped in their fall and since then wages have ceased to vary' (Rueff (1931), p. 222, translated from the French and reported in Benjamin and Kochin (1979a), n. 44).

Rueff's espousal of a link between high real wages and unemployment was widely accepted. W. H. Beveridge, for example, reproduced Rueff's key chart without significant criticism (Beveridge, 1930, p. 370). High real wages also played a pivotal rôle in Pigou's discussion of inter-war unemployment (Pigou, 1927). And Keynes later argued that Rueff's finding of a positive association between high wages and unemployment was one of the reasons why this association was part of his *General Theory* (Keynes, 1936).

Clay, Pigou and Keynes Weigh In

Initially, even Rueff's contention that high unemployment benefits were responsible for keeping wages high received significant support. As Henry Clay noted in contrasting the attitudes of inter-war workers with the views of pre-war workers:

> 'Today things are different. Successful resistance to a reduction [in wages] may still involve unemployment, but unemployment does not involve the same certainty or degree of distress. Before the war the provision of unemployment relief was partial and inadequate. Today there is a system of unemployment relief that covers all industries that are liable to serious unemployment' (Clay, 1929b, p. 335).

Pigou (1927) was even more explicit in his support of Rueff, going so far as to include an estimate of the impact on the unemployment rate:

> '. . . partly through direct State action, and partly through the added strength given to workpeoples' organisations engaged in wage bargaining by the development of unemployment insurance, wage-rates have, over a wide area, been set at a level which is too high . . . the very large percentage of unemployment which has prevailed during the whole of the last six years is due in considerable measure to this new factor . . . On a broad view of the facts, however, when all allowance has been made . . . there remains, I suggest, at least 5 per cent of extra unemployment which it is reasonable to attribute to the maintenance of rates of real wages above the level that would establish equilibrium between the demand for and supply of labour.' (Pigou, 1927, pp. 355-57.)

Even Keynes, whose *General Theory* ultimately supplanted all other explanations for the high inter-war unemployment, found Rueff's rôle for the dole appealing:

> 'I cannot help feeling that we must partly attribute to the dole the extraordinary fact—at present it is an extraordinary fact— that, in spite of the fall in prices, and the fall in the cost of living and the heavy unemployment, wages have not fallen at all since 1924' (Keynes, *Collected Writings*, Vol. XX, 1981, pp. 314-15).

Despite this early support, Rueff's insight into the importance of the insurance system was soon dismissed, largely due to expositional flaws in his argument. First, Rueff insisted that unions were playing a pivotal rôle in the process of translating high unemployment benefits into wage rigidity and thus high unemployment. Yet union membership peaked at about 45 per cent of the labour force in 1920 and declined through most of the inter-war period. Why did the growing non-union sector fail to absorb the unemployed?

In the depression of 1920-21, when the union share of the labour force was nearly double that of 1930-31, nominal wages fell swiftly. In 1930-31 wages remained nearly constant, despite an unemployment rate that was much higher. If unions were pivotal, wages should have declined more in 1931 than in 1921. Moreover, if union obstinacy was the cause of high unemployment, one would expect to find the highest unemployment in industries where unions had been most successful in keeping wages up. In fact, as even the sympathetic Henry Clay (1928) pointed out, industries where relative wages had risen the most from 1914 to 1927 had the *lowest* unemployment rates in 1927.[1]

Rueff's explanation of the importance of benefits in leading to high unemployment was also dismissed because of the rather naïve link he posited between benefits and the unemployment rate. He argued that the insurance system's effects would manifest themselves in *long-term* unemployment among persons whose wages were not much above or even *below* the level of unemployment benefits. Such a position made it easy for observers who admitted the *potential* effects of the system to dismiss the *actual* effects as insignificant. A striking example of this is found in Burns (1941). After conducting an exhaustive study of the inter-war insurance system, she concludes that unemployment insurance did not significantly add to unemployment because (i) less than 1 per cent of male applicants and 3 per cent of female applicants received benefits higher than their previous wages, and (ii) 95 per cent of the males received benefits at least 4 shillings per week less than their previous wages.[2] Another example is found in the Final Report of the Royal Commission on Unemployment Insurance (1932a). The Commission concluded that unemployment benefits had only a small effect on the unemployment rate because less than 10 per cent of the unemployed had been receiving benefits continuously for more than a year.[3]

---

[1] Each of these arguments disputed only the mechanism—union behaviour—by which benefits might have been translated into higher unemployment, not the issue of whether or not benefits did, in fact, lead to higher unemployment.

[2] Burns (1941), p. 257.

[3] Royal Commission (1932a), p. 125.

Sadly, both Burns and the Royal Commission focussed on Rueff's unfortunate straw-man argument without grappling with its essence. Burns's reasoning that people choose unemployment only if insurance benefits exceed wages is equivalent to assuming that people place a value of *zero* on their leisure time. In effect, her approach suggests that we study the effects of a fall in the price of Rolls-Royce motor cars by determining how many people now find them to be the least expensive form of transport. Similarly, in basing its conclusion about the effects of the system solely on the incidence of long-term unemployment, the Royal Commission forgot that prolonged unemployment is only one manifestation of the effects of unemployment insurance; to suppose that it is the *only* effect is equivalent to supposing that the only effect of a decline in the price of fresh produce is found in the behaviour of people who consequently adopt strict vegetarianism.

Cannan's Exposition

In essence, therefore, Rueff's underlying hypothesis—that lowering the cost of unemployment will induce more people to choose unemployment—was rejected chiefly because his posited mode of action could be shown to be flawed. Edwin Cannan's exposition of the effects of the system suffered from no such flaw. He noted, for example, that the insurance system raised the incidence of lay-offs as a substitute for hoarded labour, and acted as a subsidy to those industries whose workers could most easily maintain their eligibility:

> 'To throw large numbers of your employees out for short intervals to suit your convenience is obviously less likely to create friction, and is therefore more likely to be profitable, when the persons thrown out can draw on a common fund raised by stamp duties on employment and other taxes' (Cannan, 1930, p. 46).

Cannan also explained how the insurance system increased unemployment by increasing the amount of job search:

> '[E]specially in the occupations in which the superiority of employment over unemployment is the least, the insurance scheme has reduced the economic pressure which used to make persons grab at every chance of employment. . . . [T]he magnitude of the turnover of labour . . . is so great that a very little average delay

> will make a very large addition to the unemployment' (Cannan, 1930, pp. 46-47).

Moreover, while Cannan did not dispute the usefulness of insurance *per se*, he was concerned that the inter-war system seemed to be an excessively costly method of protecting the unemployed from destitution:

> 'The endowment of unemployment isn't made any better by calling it insurance: fire insurance wouldn't do if you let people set their property on fire and keep it burning on condition of signing their names once a week at the insurance office' (Cannan, 1928, p. 398).

Winston Churchill shared Cannan's concerns in this regard. Although Churchill defended the system as established in 1913, he believed that the inter-war system had been so liberalised as to produce an inflation of the unemployment figures:

> 'But now every case of unemployment, even for short periods, is recorded in the national register, and the benefit is increasingly applied for, even by those not in actual want, . . . as a contribution toward what may be little more than a needed holiday after years of continuous work. . . . It is significant that after every public holiday—Christmas, Easter, Whitsuntide—there is a very large addition to the unemployment total, which falls off again a few weeks later' (Churchill, 1930, p. 7).

Cannan's and Churchill's Insights Dismissed

The insights of Cannan and Churchill have been largely ignored or dismissed out of hand. Oddly, dismissal was based on the notion that anyone arguing that the system led to more unemployment must necessarily be advocating its abolition. Thus, Cannan was attacked as being 'harsh' and lacking in compassion (Hancock, 1960; Winch, 1969, Ch. 6).[1] The hypothesis that the system induced additional unemployment also met with objections on the ground that it assumed that the unemployed did not want to work (Winch, 1969). In fact, Cannan and Churchill assumed only that leisure is like any good—more of it is consumed when the cost of doing so is reduced. Moreover,

[1] As we shall see, much the same tack was taken in dismissing those observers who argued that the New Deal relief programmes raised unemployment in America.

both recognised that a principal manifestation of the added unemployment was not chronic, prolonged joblessness, but rather frequent short spells of unemployment, often for only a few days. OXO schemes enjoyed widespread popularity precisely because they offered such a convenient means of exploiting the government's subsidy to unemployment.

By the middle of the thirties, the debate over the insurance system's effects was largely over. The perceived defects in the arguments espoused by Rueff, Cannan and others, combined with the world-wide spread of high unemployment, led observers to look elsewhere for explanations. Keynes's *General Theory* seemed to be just the ticket, offering both diagnosis—deficit aggregate demand—and remedy—deficit spending. And once this approach was adopted, the insurance system disappeared from view in discussions of the unemployment problem.

2. Unemployment Relief in Inter-War America

(a) The Essentials

Like Britain until shortly before the First World War, America had no centrally financed or administered assistance for the unemployed until the 1930s. Numerous local governments had modest programmes to aid people in financial straits, and in some cases localities were assisted by state governments in these endeavours. In addition, there were privately funded charitable organisations to aid the destitute, and some labour unions provided assistance for members with financial troubles. In each of these programmes, however, the criterion for assistance was need-based, and unemployment *per se* was neither a necessary nor a sufficient condition for assistance to be forthcoming; in all cases, the central government remained a passive spectator.

The unprecedented unemployment and financial hardships of the Great Depression brought forth a considerable expansion of relief activities by local governments, private organisations and, to a lesser extent, state governments. Initially, however, the national government remained content merely to encourage such efforts. It was not until 1932, with the establishment of the Reconstruction Finance Corporation (RFC), that the national government played any direct rôle in relief. The RFC was created and authorised by Congress to issue $300 million in bonds, the proceeds of which were to be distributed to state governments that had exhausted their own relief resources. The states, in turn, were to lend the RFC-provided funds to private firms who were otherwise unable to obtain credit. In practice, states found it difficult to convince the national government they had exhausted their own resources, so that distribution of RFC monies was slow; by the end of 1932 only about $100 million had been distributed.[1] In any event, funds were disbursed by the states in the form of loans to private businesses, rather than in direct grants to individuals who might be unemployed or in financial distress.

In 1933, newly elected President Roosevelt quickly supplanted the RFC with the Federal Emergency Relief Administration (FERA), which was to spend $3 billion on the relief of unemployment. FERA represented a fundamental change in philosophy from the RFC, and a precursor of the relief efforts that were to follow over the next seven years.

- First, there was its sheer magnitude: on an annualised basis, its budget was five times as large as the RFC's had been.
- Second, FERA was established to get financial assistance directly into the hands of unemployed individuals, through a combination of cash grants and work relief.
- Third, FERA was truly 'federal' in its administration, involving both funding and personnel supplied at the national, state, and local government levels.

The FERA programme was *not* an unemployment insurance system. Funding, for example, came not from contributions or premiums paid by employers and employees, but from the general revenues of the various governments. Moreover, there were no statutory benefit levels *per se*. Instead, 'need levels' were established by local officials; people whose incomes fell below these standards were eligible to receive FERA funds equal to the difference between their incomes and the operative local need levels. Formally, unemployment *per se* was neither necessary nor

---

[1] One important reason the states had trouble convincing the national government that they had exhausted their relief resources was that most states did not even have relief programmes prior to 1933.

sufficient for an individual to receive FERA money; operationally, it was frequently both. Employment earnings were effectively taxed at a 100 per cent rate, via offsets to relief benefits, and a full-time worker with earnings close to the local average was unlikely to qualify for benefits, unless he had a particularly large family. Recipients of FERA benefits were occasionally required to perform public service work for local governments, but it was far more commonplace for there to be no work requirements.

'Work Relief' under the WPA

FERA began to be phased out late in 1935 by the inception of the Works Progress Administration (WPA), a programme that explicitly established a system of 'work relief' on a nation-wide level. As under FERA, need levels were set by local officials, who also established 'pay schedules' for various occupations. The able-bodied unemployed who had usable skills were expected to work on government projects for a number of hours each month that, when multiplied by the locally determined rate of pay for their occupation, would equal the cash payment to which their need level entitled them. Thus, if a person's need level called for a monthly WPA payment of $60 and if the local pay for that person's occupation was $0·60 per hour, then 100 hours of work per month would be required. It was also recognised, however, that some people would be unable to work or would have skills unsuitable for the WPA projects contemplated; they became eligible for 'general relief', which entailed an unconditional monthly cash grant equal to the difference between their need level and their income. This combination of work relief and general relief remained in effect until the onset of the Second World War, with about one-half of recipients employed on WPA projects (such as building post offices and bridges) and one-half on general relief.

Although FERA and the WPA were both designed chiefly to aid the unemployed, there was an important conceptual difference between the two programmes. FERA's principal goal was to get money into the hands of the unemployed and the destitute as quickly as possible, with little regard for services that might be rendered in return. The WPA, however, sought explicitly to obtain labour services in return for relief payments.

Neither an inability to work nor a lack of usable skills was a formal bar to the receipt of relief benefits, for there remained the possibility of receiving general relief; nevertheless, an able-bodied individual with usable skills was expected to work in return for relief assistance, and a refusal to comply was deemed sufficient grounds for denial of relief benefits.

Despite the WPA emphasis on work relief, the administration of FERA and the WPA was otherwise remarkably similar. State governors, in consultation with local authorities, submitted budget requests to national administrators in Washington DC. These administrators approved the budget requests in whole or in part and disbursed funds to the governors, who in turn distributed funds to their local governments. On average, about 80 per cent of relief funds were provided by the national government, with the bulk of the remainder coming from state governments. In essence, the national government provided most of the funding, the state governments co-ordinated the requests of local governments and served as a conduit for funding, and the local governments decided which individuals would receive relief and how much aid each would receive. Under this system, it was commonplace for local authorities wholly to exhaust their monthly budgets before all applicants had been funded—a fact that is of some importance in our subsequent analysis of the effects of the relief system.

(b) Some Unusual Features

Both FERA and the WPA embodied distinctive features that shaped the impact of the programmes and thus have influenced our analysis. Here we sketch the major points of each feature, noting their salient implications.

(i) The Federal System and the Budget Process

We noted earlier that both FERA and the WPA were, strictly speaking, federal efforts, in that both personnel and funding came from national, state, and local governments in a co-operative effort to relieve the hardship of the unemployed. In point of fact, however, the financing for these programmes was driven, either directly or indirectly, almost exclusively by decisions made in Washington DC, by officials of the national government. Most of the funding under FERA and the WPA came from the national government, and most state funding was forthcoming only in response to offers of matching funds from the national government; prior to the offer of matching funds under FERA, for example, only seven out of 48 states had relief programmes operating at the state level.[1]

As a practical matter, then, decisions about funding levels were made at the national level. In contrast, the day-to-day administration of FERA and the WPA was in the hands of local officials. They determined who was eligible for relief funds; they decided on local need levels and thus the local benefit levels; and it was local officials who decided which applicants would work in return for their benefits and what 'wage' they would be paid for that work.

This separation of the funding and the disbursement of relief monies made FERA and WPA funds appear to be largely 'free money' from the perspective of local officials. FERA and WPA funds from the national and state governments could not be used to reduce local taxes nor increase spending on non-relief activities.[2] Thus, local officials had an incentive to determine eligibility and need levels so as completely to exhaust their relief budgets. This incentive was magnified by the fact that local governments which did not exhaust their budgets in a given budget cycle were typically given less money in subsequent cycles. Had the budget cycle been sufficiently long, this 'spend it or lose it' approach to funding might have been of little consequence. However, while national funding for FERA was appropriated on an annual basis, and the initial funds for WPA came in a multi-year lump-sum appropriation, local relief officials were forced to follow a *monthly* budget cycle. Each month, they were required to submit budget requests based on the then current conditions; these requests were collated and forwarded to Washington by state officials; and each month national relief officials decided funding levels for the states and thus the localities.

---

[1] Many states did not even offer to serve as conduits for RFC loans until after FERA was established and states were told that RFC monies could be used as matching funds for FERA grants from the national government.

[2] It was possible for local governments to contribute their own funds to FERA and WPA relief; however, national officials were prone simply to cut back on national funds in response. Needless to say, locally-provided funds quickly dried up.

Population was an important criterion in decisions at the national level about FERA and WPA funding levels, and this was a criterion which introduced substantial stability in the monthly allocations. Nevertheless, variation in the other factors taken into account at the national level was large enough to produce substantial variation in *per capita* funding levels from one month to the next. As a result, local officials found themselves each month with a *de facto* base level allocation that depended on population, and a substantial residual component that fluctuated considerably. In response, local officials altered both need levels and eligibility requirements frequently, depending on the exact size of their budget in any month. A large budget typically was translated into (i) an increase in the number of persons deemed eligible for relief, and (ii) higher benefits per person. Smaller budget allocations from Washington produced more stringent eligibility requirements and lower benefits per recipient. As a practical matter, therefore, eligibility requirements and benefit levels were fine-tuned by local officials on a monthly basis to exhaust their fluctuating budget allocations.

(ii) Measuring Benefits

As already mentioned, benefit levels were set by local officials rather than at the state or national level. Moreover, benefits payable in any given locality could and often did change from month to month, depending on current budgetary constraints. As a practical matter, therefore, the only feasible measure of the generosity of the relief programmes is the average level of benefits actually paid to recipients. Such a measure presents a potentially serious problem of measurement error.[1] To understand this problem, imagine that there are two groups of potential relief recipients and that members of one group are eligible for higher benefits than members of the other group, perhaps because the former have more dependants. Suppose also that the *composition* of people on relief depends in part on some (unmeasured) factor other than the level of benefits payable to each group. If the unmeasured factor changes so as to cause a rise in the proportion of the recipient population comprised of people

[1] See Benjamin and Kochin (1979a) and (1982) for an extended discussion of this issue.

eligible for high benefits, *measured* benefits will rise, even though the *true* benefits payable to any individual have not changed. Conversely, if a change in the unmeasured factor causes a rise in the proportion of low-benefit people in the recipient population to rise, *measured* benefits will fall, even though the true benefits payable to any individual have not changed.[1]

A classic example of the operation of such forces can be found in the inter-war British unemployment insurance system.[2] The largest cut in unemployment benefits in this period came late in 1931, when benefits for all classes of recipients were cut by 10 per cent. At the same time, regulations were promulgated that made it much more difficult for women—the low-benefit group—to obtain any benefits at all. The consequence was that even though the largest single *decline* in true benefits occurred between 1931 and 1932, *measured* average benefits exhibited their largest *increase* at that time, because so many (low-benefit) women disappeared from the ranks of the unemployed.

It is an easy matter to avoid the potential measurement error associated with the use of average benefits paid, if one has access to (i) a statutory schedule of benefits payable to various recipient groups (for example, men, women, married, single, and so on), and (ii) weights to apply to these statutory benefit levels. The resulting fixed-weight index of benefits can be highly stylised—for example, benefits payable to a married man with two children; or it can be more 'realistic', reflecting the true composition of the unemployed at a point in time—for example, 0·27 single men, 0·14 married men, 0·19 women, and so on. The essential features of the index are that (i) it employs fixed weights, and (ii) it is highly correlated with 'true' benefits.

In the case of the relief programmes of the thirties in America, the construction of a fixed benefits index is simply not feasible: there were literally thousands of different need levels (and thus

---

[1] If the unmeasured factor causes compositional changes that are uncorrelated with true benefits, the only impact of using average benefits paid will be to introduce measurement error, thereby biasing downward the estimated impact of benefits on unemployment. If compositional changes and true benefits are correlated, this downward bias in the estimated coefficient of benefits may be either amplified or mitigated, depending on whether the correlation is negative or positive.

[2] See Benjamin and Kochin (1979a) and (1982).

benefit rates) at any point in time, and these need levels frequently changed from one month to the next in response to budgetary pressures. Moreover, although we know the average number of dependants per relief recipient, we have no other comprehensive data on the composition of the recipient population, either cross-sectionally or across time. Thus, we are forced to use average benefits actually paid as our measure of the attractiveness of the relief system.

Fortunately, the operation of the system was such that the potential bias introduced by using average benefits paid is probably small. As noted above, local governments operated on a monthly budget cycle; it appears that responses to increases (decreases) in monthly budget allocations took the form of roughly across-the-board increases (decreases) in need levels, and increases (decreases) in the proportion of applicants who were served. We have found no evidence that such changes led to systematic changes in the composition of recipients. Similarly, across different states and localities, budget allocations seem to have been driven by factors such as total population and geographic and political considerations that would not be expected to be related to the composition of recipients. When combined with the fact that there appear to have been no major administrative changes (such as occurred in Britain) that would be expected to produce pronounced changes in the composition of recipients, these features are such that the worst damage done by the use of average benefits rather than fixed-weight benefits may be a modest downward bias in the estimated impact of the relief system on private employment.

(iii) The Method of Counting

As discussed earlier, the unit of counting the number of persons receiving financial assistance under the provisions of the inter-war British system was the number of insurance books lodged with the Employment Exchanges. Each book corresponded to one unemployed person.[1] In the relief programmes of inter-war

[1] We abstract here from those unemployed people who did not have lodged books—either because they typically worked in uninsured industries, or because they were not collecting benefits and did not wish to avail themselves of the job placement services of the Employment Exchanges. Such people, of course, would not in any event have been among the counted unemployed.

America, the unit of counting was the 'case'—typically a family unit, which could consist of one or many individuals. Since unemployment was neither a necessary nor a sufficient condition for the receipt of relief, a relief case might correspond to zero, one, two, or more unemployed persons. To understand this, consider four examples, each of which would count as one relief case:

- a working single woman with minor dependent children;
- a non-working single woman with minor dependent children, whose value in the job market is less than her value at home;
- an unemployed, able-bodied man whose spouse's value at home exceeds her value in the job market; and
- a man, woman and juvenile son/daughter living at home, all able-bodied but unemployed.

In the first example, both a relief case and an employed person would be present in the data. In the second, there would be a relief case, but no associated unemployment. In the third, the correspondence between the case count and the number of unemployed would be exact. In the final example, one relief case would correspond to *three* unemployed persons.

The importance of the method of counting under the American system is simple: knowing the number of relief cases may be an overstatement or an understatement of the number of unemployed people. More generally, even the knowledge that an X per cent increase in relief benefits per case led to a Y per cent increase in the number of cases does not directly lead to an estimate of the response of *employment* to an increase in relief benefits. Additional relief cases may be associated with *no change* in employment, or with an impact on employment that is *larger* in number. As will become apparent in Chapter 5, this consideration has played a major rôle in our approach to estimating the effects of the relief system in inter-war America.

APPENDIX TO CHAPTER 3

Measuring Wages

In preparing the estimates of the structural model of the labour market in the UK, we have used the average earnings figures produced by Feinstein (1972). In using an average estimate we recognise the many problems associated with the measurement of wages. At the conceptual level, average weekly earnings differ from wages in that the latter fails to account for actual hours worked. Given the preponderance of short-time during the inter-war period, we would expect considerable differences between the series. However, as Table A.3:1 shows, despite the differences in coverage, the movement of wage-rates and earnings presented in Feinstein (1972, T140) was broadly similar.[1]

Econometricians and labour economists, estimating labour supply functions, would favour the use of weekly wage-rates rather than earnings, as the latter include elements of the supply decision. But this assumes that the supply decision is not influenced by 'normal' income, which would include a certain amount of overtime or, in the case of the inter-war period, an expected amount of short-time. Furthermore, it can be argued that the decision between work and leisure depends on the ratio of weekly benefits to 'normal' weekly income. These arguments are, however, somewhat academic given that the available series move so closely together.

An alternative criticism is the use of the Feinstein index of earnings of wage earners instead of annual average earnings (wages and salaries excluding directors' fees) used by Benjamin and Kochin (1979a). Both series derive from Chapman and Knight (1953) and are depicted in Chart A.3:1. The difference reflects the fact that (higher-paid and largely insurance-exempt) salaried workers are included in the Benjamin and Kochin estimates. The average earnings figures are around 19 per cent higher than the wage earnings figures. Since unemployment benefits are likely to have had more of an effect on insured wage earners (at least prior to Unemployment Assistance), this suggests that, if anything, Benjamin and Kochin may have under-

---

[1] The available average weekly wage-rates from Feinstein (1972, p. T140) are based on the Ramsbottom (1935, 1938, 1939) index and taken from Chapman and Knight (1953).

TABLE A.3:1

WEEKLY WAGE-RATES AND EARNINGS IN THE UK: AVERAGE ANNUAL INCREASE, 1921-23 TO 1936-38

	Average Weekly Wage Rates %	Average Weekly Wage Earnings %
1921-23	-11·4	-11·2
1924-26	0·9	0·0
1927-29	-0·9	0·4
1930-32	-1·1	-1·7
1933-35	0·0	-0·5
1936-38	2·9	3·3

estimated the average replacement rate for this period. However, this contention cannot be sustained. An alternative estimate of wages is produced by the Ministry of Labour (*Ministry of Labour Gazette*, 1924, 1928, 1931, 1935, and 1938) via an October survey of the normal weekly wage of manual workers. Taking 1935 as an illustration, the Chapman figure for weekly earnings (wages and salaries) is 55*s* (shillings) while the wage earnings figure is 46*s* 3*d*

Chart A.3.1:
Average Earnings in the UK, 1920-38
(1920 = 100)

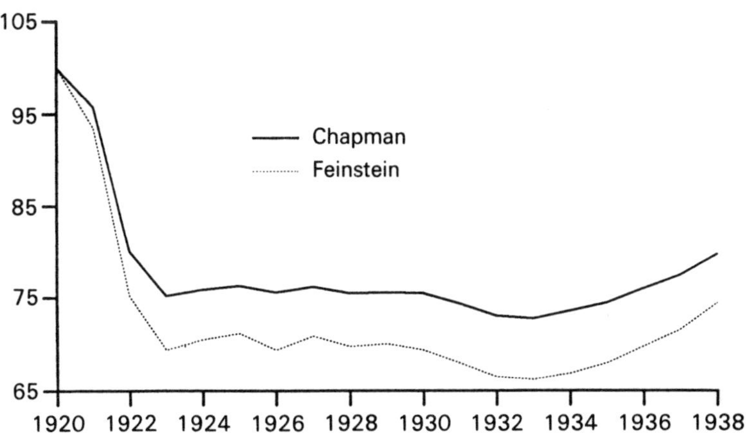

and the Ministry of Labour figure is 48*s* 11*d*. The latter two figures are fairly close, given that Chapman's estimates are for a year as a whole whereas the Ministry figures are based on the October survey. Both the Ministry figure and Chapman's figure can be thought of as being made up of three wage components:

(i) the wages of men over 21;

(ii) the wages of women over 18; and

(iii) the wages of juveniles and younger people.

Since benefits affected principally the adult population, we can consider men over 21 and women over 18 as the 'population at risk'. A calculation of the average wage of the population at risk in October 1935 produces an estimate of 56*s* 8*d*—a figure close to the Chapman earnings (wages and salaries) estimate. Again, this figure is an *average*, and as such the replacement rate will depend on the distribution of adult manual workers both by region and by industry. Tables 5 and 6 in Chapter 4 show that these considerations are significant. Clearly the choice of series will matter to the estimate of the replacement rate. However, given that the correlation coefficient between the average earnings and average wage earnings series is 0·984, it is unlikely that the choice will significantly matter for the wage equations presented in Chapter 4.

This discussion highlights the important consideration of aggregation. Using time-series data for the UK means that we were unable properly to address this problem. Thankfully, this problem is partially dealt with in the data for the United States. Table A.3:2 shows the inter-industry distribution of average monthly earnings from official sources against the unweighted average of the wages of 48 states from our sample.

The low figures in the last column arise because the average is not weighted by population and therefore gives disproportionate weight to the farming states of the South and Mid-West. The use of pooled cross-section time-series data takes into account the distribution of average wages across states, and since individual states are dominated by particular industries, the estimates will to some extent take into account the inter-industry distribution of wages.

Finally, because we wished to keep econometric estimation to

TABLE A.3:2
AVERAGE MONTHLY WAGES IN THE USA, 1933-35 TO 1939
(US dollars)

	All Industries	Manufacturing	Agriculture	Average of 48 States
1933-35	91·14	96·05	21·07	77·06
1936-38	102·12	110·07	26·72	89·61
1939	105·3	113·5	32·08	92·74

a minimum, we did not address the question: Real wages to whom—employers or employees? The real wage to employers is labour cost (inclusive of employer's labour taxes such as insurance contributions) deflated by the product price, whereas the real wage to the employee is the net wage (net of insurance contributions) deflated by the consumption goods price. Chart A.3:2 shows how differently these two series have moved during this period for the UK. The wage data are average annual earnings in manufacturing. The deflators are the wholesale price index and the retail price index (both 1924 = 100: Capie and

Chart A.3.2:
Real Wages in the UK, 1920-38
(Logarithmic Scale)

Collins, 1983). Employers' real labour costs are defined as wages plus employers' contributions deflated by the wholesale price index, whereas real wages to employees are wages deflated by the retail price index. The divergence of the two series illustrates the extent to which employers' real labour costs rose in the latter half of the inter-war years. It follows that the estimates of the wage elasticity of labour demand produced in our study are probably understated. This means that the effect of supply factors such as benefits had possibly even a greater effect than that suggested in this study.

4

RIOTOUS ASSEMBLY

Introduction

WE HAVE ALREADY STATED that the emergence of prolonged mass unemployment is perhaps the best remembered historical phenomenon of the inter-war years. Most people remember the inter-war period, particularly the decade of the thirties, in terms of hunger marches, soup kitchens, dole queues and red banners proclaiming the 'Right to Work'. The popular image of the period is one of poverty and deprivation, caused by the denial of work. Mention the period between the wars and to most people the immediate image is of the 'Hungry Thirties'. So powerful is this view of the period that any attempt at a dispassionate study of unemployment usually evokes more heat than light.

In a trivial sense, of course, it can always be argued that unemployment is caused by an excess supply of labour, but such a statement is uninformative, because it tells us nothing about what has caused the excess supply, and more importantly, why wage adjustments fail to bring the labour market into equilibrium. The consensus view of inter-war Britain is of a period plagued by recurrent negative demand shocks, culminating in a collapse of economic activity following the 1929 crash of the US stock market, and the subsequent downturn in world trade.[1] The

[1] In the UK, the act of returning to the Gold Standard in 1925 was a source of additional deflationary pressure by over-valuing the currency; see, for instance, Moggridge (1969). This view has, however, been challenged by Sayers (1969) and more recently by Matthews (1986b, 1989a).

portrait of America is that of a land of plenty suddenly swept into a decade of privation by a depression of staggering severity. No credible commentator would question the notion that the inter-war British and American economies were subjected to reductions in aggregate demand of historic proportions. The real issue that divides economists lies in their explanations for the failure of wages to respond adequately to these shocks.

To Keynesians, sticky money wages are unsurprising, even in the face of prolonged unemployment. Money illusion, faulty expectations, long-term contracts, worker concerns over the 'hierarchy' of relative wages, or some combination of all of these, are seen as commonplace features of the world. Any fall in nominal demand in the presence of such factors leads to a rise in real wages and an increase in unemployment that is likely to persist until an offsetting increase in demand occurs. In contrast, the Classical approach emphasises an equilibrium framework of analysis. Unanticipated nominal shocks can alter real wages in the short run, but once (rational) expectations and (efficient) contractual arrangements respond, money wages will adjust fully to their new equilibrium level. Any prolonged failure of real wages to restore 'full employment', it is argued, must be due to real supply factors defining a new equilibrium position. Here the Classical economist will appeal to real wage rigidities created by trade union behaviour, minimum wage legislation or unemployment benefits.[1]

The debate between proponents of the Keynesian and Classical positions occupied a prominent place in the inter-war economic literature on both sides of the Atlantic. This spirited 'war of the words' became a Keynesian rout, however, with the publication of *The General Theory*, and the Classical view quickly disappeared from view. After the Second World War, a resurgence of interest in the Classical approach was ultimately applied to the US experience by Darby (1976) and to the British experience by Benjamin and Kochin (1979a). These papers,

[1] A third approach to explaining the prolonged unemployment of the inter-war years relies on factors unique as to time and place. Largely devoid of predictive content, this 'structural' approach will be discussed only briefly in what follows.

particularly the latter, have stimulated a vigorous renewal of the long-dormant inter-war debate.[1] Our purpose in this chapter is to sketch the highlights of the debate over inter-war unemployment, from its origins up to the current state of play. This sketch will lay the groundwork for the new empirical results presented in Chapter 5.

1. The Classical View

At the outset, it is important to be clear on one point: the emergence of unemployment in response to a negative demand shock was no mystery to the classical economists of the inter-war period. Thus, when monetary restriction was begun in 1920, few contemporary economists were surprised to see the unemployment rate rise rapidly. Cannan, Fisher, Keynes, and others were cognisant that few prices were perfectly flexible; as a result, they recognised that a general deflation would be accompanied by an industrial crisis. A temporary increase in unemployment was simply the price to be paid if inflation was to be reversed. What was puzzling was the emergence of prolonged high unemployment, for despite a vigorous economic expansion the unemployment rate refused to fall below 10 per cent.

Although the Classical attempt to explain this puzzle had many facets, the inter-war system of unemployment insurance played an early and recurrent rôle. Perhaps the simplest rôle for the system was based on the fact that most people find leisure preferable to work. Anything, such as unemployment benefits, which made leisure more attractive than work would induce people to consume more leisure and work less. Thus, as discussed in Chapter 3, Jacques Rueff argued that the insurance system made unemployment a superior alternative to employment available at wages little if any higher than unemployment benefits.

There were more subtle applications of the principle that lowering the cost of an activity will lead to more of that activity. Edwin Cannan, for example, recognised that, even in the best of

[1] For instance, Metcalf *et al.* (1982), Cross (1982), Collins (1982), and Ormerod and Worswick (1982).

times, few workers immediately found new work after leaving their old job. Instead, they typically spent some period of time looking for new employment that both matched their skills and offered a suitable wage-rate. The cost to the individual of such search consists of both out-of-pocket costs and the wages forgone while unemployed. Cannan recognised that any system of unemployment insurance reduces these costs by reducing the net income forgone during search. Thus, workers search longer for jobs, which in turn increases the measured unemployment rate.

Cannan also recognised that the system induced employers to substitute lay-offs for hoarded labour, and acted as a subsidy to those industries whose workers could most easily maintain their eligibility.

Short-time Working—the OXO System

As we noted in Chapter 3 (above, pp. 49-50), the joint incentive of employer and employee to take maximum advantage of the subsidy provided by the insurance system reached its full fruition in the widespread adoption of short-time work schemes, such as the OXO system. Such arrangements were of concern to Cannan not because he disputed the usefulness of insurance *per se*, but because the inter-war system seemed to be an excessively costly method of protecting the unemployed from destitution. (For an analysis of the incentive structure of the OXO scheme, see Box 1, below, pp. 78-79.)

Winston Churchill shared Cannan's concerns in this regard. Although Churchill defended the system as established in 1913, he believed that the inter-war system had been so liberalised as to produce an inflation of the unemployment figures.

Trade unions played a key rôle in the arguments of several observers seeking to explain the failure of wage adjustments to bring about normal levels of unemployment. Rueff, for example, argued that high unemployment benefits encouraged trade unions to resist cuts in nominal wages, regardless of the level of unemployment among their members. The result was higher unemployment.

Both the size of the union sector and the operation of trade boards in fixing minimum wages were emphasised by Clay (1929b) in explaining the downward rigidity of wages. He estimated that in 1925, 1·5 million workers had their wages regulated by trade boards acting under the auspices of the Minimum Wages Acts of 1909 and 1918. Other informal and semi-official authorities that took their lead from the trade boards and the agricultural wages boards, such as the Whitley scheme in the railway industry, brought the total affected by trade board rulings to about 8 million workers, nearly one-half of the total work-force. Clay also noted that while union membership had fallen during the twenties, it had grown from 2·5 million in 1914 to 8·3 million in 1920, and was still 4·9 million in 1927. This meant that although the union 'mark-up' may have weakened during the twenties, it was still significant compared with its pre-war position. The rôle of unemployment benefits was to buttress the bargaining position of unions and to discourage non-union workers from accepting wage cuts.

Money-Wage Stickiness: Pigou's Four Arguments

Although a similar view was taken by Pigou, his broader view on the issue of money-wage stickiness went well beyond a concern over the influence of the unemployment insurance system. In his evidence to the Macmillan Committee on Finance and Industry (1931), for example, he produced four arguments relating to the problem of money-wage stickiness.

- *First*, following a line normally associated with the Keynesian view, Pigou thought that workers might resist wage cuts out of fear that they would lose ground relative to workers who successfully resisted such cuts.

- *Second*, he argued that worker truculence over wage cuts could arise because of a perception that real wages were already too low.

- *Third*, resistance could be attributed to worker uncertainty over whether a cut in money wages when prices fell would be reversed when prices rose.

- *Fourth*, and significantly, Pigou acknowledged the importance of expectations in guiding workers' wage demands. Although he rejected money illusion, Pigou clearly recognised the

BOX 1

Short-time Working

The *incentives* to short-time working in the 1930s are examined briefly in this note. The OXO system allowed someone to collect daily benefit if he worked three days less, in a six-day week. The binding constraint was three days work. If this was breached, the worker was disqualified from benefit. Three cases are analysed: (i) the person who prefers to work three days on and three days off; (ii) the person who prefers to work less than three days; and (iii) the person who wishes to continue working a full week.

Let the normal working week be given by KL in Figure B.1:1, and for argument's sake, let us say that the amount of wage income earned in the normal working week (OY) coincides with the individual's optimum position P. The level of income available in full unemployment is the benefit rate given by OB. If the maximum amount of time a person can work, without disqualifying himself from benefit, is three in six days, then HL is ½KL and wage income would be OV = ½OY. Because the worker can claim daily unemployment benefits for the days he did not work, to a maximum of three in six days, the actual income-leisure trade-off he faces is described by CQSW.

If the worker works one day and is unemployed for five days he receives his daily wage plus ⅚ths of the weekly benefit. If he works two days he receives ⅓rd of his weekly wage plus ⅔rds of his weekly benefit, and if he works three days he gets ½ of his weekly wage and ½ of weekly benefits. Thus QH is larger than OV. Now, if he works four days he receives ⅔rds of his weekly pay and no benefits. Given this incentive structure we can distinguish between three types of worker, two who would prefer to work on short-time (one of these would at least be indifferent) and one who would not.

existence of a temporary trade-off between unanticipated inflation and unemployment, thereby pre-dating the Friedman/Phelps expectations-augmented Phillips curve:

> '. . . devices such as devaluation, and inflation, and so on act only in so far as the wage earners are, so to speak, bamboozled. If a workman realises that the raising of prices through inflation is going to hit him he will normally ask for an increase in money wages corresponding to the rise in prices . . .' (Pigou, 1931, Evidence to the Macmillan Committee, p. 58, s. 6151.)

Figure B.1.1

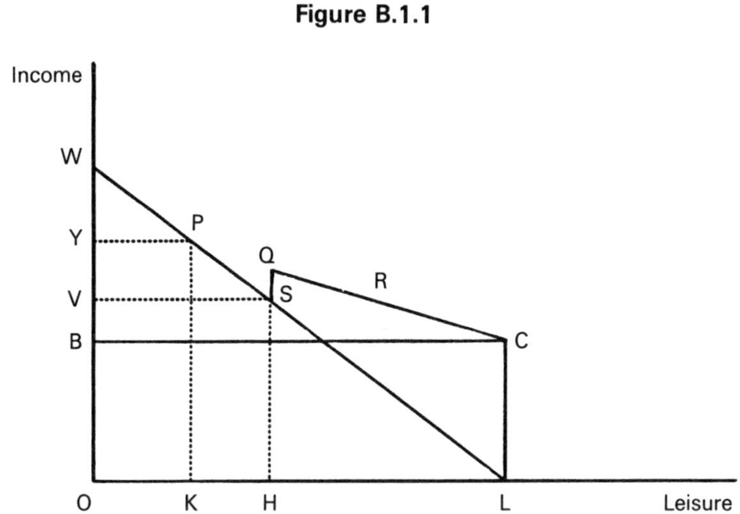

The high income-low leisure preferer would conceivably remain at P. The point Q would be preferable to those who attach a higher premium to leisure (at the very least they would be indifferent between P and Q). Finally, for those who have a stronger preference for leisure, some point between Q and C would be the optimal point (say, R). Thus anyone on short-time anywhere in the range QC would be better off (or at least indifferent) in terms of individual welfare. Any one who worked more than HL units (three days) would be worse off, in terms of individual welfare. This explains both the attractiveness and the popularity of the 'three on the book and three on the hook' organisation of short-time working.

Above all this, however, Pigou was careful to include the rôle of benefits as a source of wage rigidity:

> 'All these are reasons for what you may call stickiness in money rates of wages. Further, these resistances are strengthened and made more effective by the unemployment insurance system. If that was not there, the pressure to accept a reduction of money wages when there was a lot of unemployment would be much stronger than it is now.' (Pigou, 1931 Evidence, *ibid.*, p. 84, s. 6552.)

The underlying thread of Pigou's analysis—that unemployment insurance acted as a distortion, strengthening the power of the unions in resisting wage cuts and effectively placing a floor on the real wage—was in line with that of many of his contemporaries. The prevalence of this view is indicated in the following extract from the *Report of Committee of Economists* in October 1930 (reprinted in Howson and Winch, 1977):

> 'Before the War, if unemployment in any industry went beyond a certain point, it was in the interests of the trade unions to modify wage-rates. To-day, the existence of the unemployment insurance system, divorced as it has become from any actuarial basis, is tending to prevent these adjustments. Yet if such adjustments are not made, it is a matter of common experience that unemployment follows.' (Howson and Winch, 1977, p. 183.)

Ironically, although Keynes, a member of the Committee, chose to emphasise factors such as the world slump and the influence of domestic demand in causing high unemployment, as noted in Chapter 3, he clearly recognised the effect unemployment benefits had on wages:

> 'The existence of the dole undoubtedly diminishes the pressure on the individual man to accept a rate of wages or a kind of employment which is not just what he wants or what he is used to. In the old days the pressure on the unemployed was to get back somehow or other into employment, and if that was so today surely it would have more effect on the prevailing rate of wages than it has today.' (Keynes, *Collected Writings*, Vol. XX, 1981, pp. 318-19.)

The Classical diagnosis was therefore clear in its identification of the supply factors responsible for wage rigidity and prolonged unemployment in inter-war Britain. The unemployment insurance system directly induced additional unemployment by encouraging individuals to choose leisure over work, search longer between jobs, and find schemes such as OXO that maximised the subsidy to intermittent employment. Unemployment benefits also acted indirectly by buttressing union power and validating the actions of the trade boards in setting minimum wages. On both counts, the adjustment of wages in response to demand shocks was diminished, producing a rise in unemployment. Moreover, the failure of wages to adjust sufficiently meant that international competitiveness was eroded, with all of the attendant implications for exports and for employment in the traded sector.[1]

2. The Received View

Most observers have argued that the overriding principle of British government action during the early twenties was that recommended by the Cunliffe Committee (1919): the restoration of the Gold Standard. Even those who have argued that it was the authorities' fear of inflation which guided monetary policy, nevertheless accept that government policy in fact enabled the return to gold.[2] Whatever the government's underlying motives, the post-war inflationary boom was followed rapidly by depression, largely in response to the deflationary policy of the government. The traditional view of the events that followed, which we characterise as fundamentally Keynesian, is that the ensuing maintenance of a strong deflationary policy pushed the economy into the 'doldrums', culminating in the return to gold in April 1925 at the pre-war parity of $4·86. Under this view, the return to gold consolidated the slump until a new wave of deflationary shocks hit the economy following the US stock market crash and the financial crisis of 1931. The ensuing fall from gold heralded an 'era of cheap money' which contributed importantly to the (partial) recovery of the thirties. Thus, the inter-war years have been cast as suffering from chronically deficient aggregate demand.[3]

---

[1] This view is expressed clearly in the National Confederation of Employers' Organisations' (NCEO) evidence to the Royal Commission on Unemployment Insurance in May 1931. The NCEO argued that the strength of international competitiveness was such that an extra 1*d* on employers' contributions would be the margin on which contracts were gained or lost.

[2] See Morgan (1952).

[3] The supposed source of demand shocks in the second half of the twenties is not universally accepted. For instance, Sayers (1969) questions the notion that the source of the fundamental disequilibrium was an exchange rate of $4·86. His argument is that the depression in the export industries was entirely the fault of the world trade cycle and not of British monetary policy.

The popularity of the Keynesian explanation of inter-war events has been due to its apparent ability to explain the link between monetary policy, production and unemployment. The rise in the exchange rate brought about by tight monetary policy required an equivalent fall in the domestic price level, or an equivalent rise in foreign prices, if competitiveness was to be maintained. In a system with fully flexible wages and prices, such a policy would not have been a problem. A lower price level would have been matched by lower money wages and a higher nominal exchange rate. Both competitiveness and full employment would have been maintained. The Keynesian explanation for the failure of this scenario to occur centred on the failure of the price level to adjust adequately, and this in turn was linked to the failure of money wages to adjust. The consequent worsening of international competitiveness was the key contributor to the slump, according to Keynes and subsequent analysts:

> 'The major part of our trouble is the equilibrium terms of trade, having turned seriously against us, without this being compensated by a reduction in money wages to correspond to the new equilibrium terms of trade.' (Keynes, *Collected Writings*, Vol. III, 1973, p. 179.)

While recognising the link between wages and competitiveness, Keynes was unsure of its quantitative magnitude. In 1925, sterling was supposed to be over-valued by at least 10 per cent; to Keynes and his followers this represented the 'fundamental disequilibrium' that produced the relative stagnation of the economy during the second half of the twenties. Since the demand for labour is derived from the general demand for goods and services, an over-valued exchange rate and tight domestic monetary policy reduced the demand for both goods and labour, leading to an excess supply in both markets.[1]

---

[1] The traditionally gloomy view of the inter-war economy has been challenged by a school of thought which we term the 'structuralists'. This school, led by Richardson (1962) and Aldcroft (1967), challenges the view that monetary factors had more than temporary effects, and instead argues that relative changes in demand and supply, particularly long-run structural changes, explain the behaviour of the inter-war economy. According to the structuralist view, the British economy was in a better state than before the War, compared favourably with other industrial countries, and produced an infrastructure for sustained long-term growth. The only blot on the landscape was the existence

[*Cont'd. on p. 83*]

A necessary ingredient in this story was, of course, an explanation for the existence of money-wage rigidity. Many modern writers (*cf.* Leijonhufvud, 1968, and Clower, 1965) have emphasised Keynes's argument that workers possessed 'inelastic expectations': lacking complete information as to whether a negative demand shock was specific to their industry or general in nature, workers refused to accept a cut in money wages, although the existence of full information would have caused them to accept the cut. However, Keynes also recognised that institutional factors lay behind money-wage rigidity: the relative stability of the pre-war economy had produced a traditional 'hierarchy' of relative wages across occupations and industries, a hierarchy defended with particular vigour by the unions. Wage cuts were seen as a threat to this hierarchy, and were therefore resisted. The notion that 'money illusion'—an inability of workers to tell the difference between nominal wage cuts and real wage cuts—played a part in the labour market has also entered into some Keynesian explanations of inter-war wage rigidity (*cf.* Levacic, 1984), despite its inconsistency with the basic principles of economic theory.

Finally, recent research suggests that 'implicit contracts' could have played a rôle in buttressing wage rigidity: in the presence of firm-specific human capital, firms and workers will have a joint incentive to respond to demand reductions via lay-offs rather than wage cuts. Such contracts, it is argued, are more prevalent in labour markets than in product markets. Thus, nominal wages will tend to be less flexible than prices, producing a rise in real wages and unemployment when negative nominal demand shocks occur.

Keynes's Antipathy to Wage Cuts

Even if these obstacles to wage flexibility could somehow be overcome, engineered wage cuts would not, according to Keynes, produce the desired results. This would work only if the product prices remained the same or did not fall by as much. Keynes

---

of high average unemployment. Here also a structural answer was conjectured. High unemployment and chronic depression were particularly associated with the traditional (staple) export trades, such as coal, cotton, heavy engineering, shipbuilding, railways, and iron and steel, in which Britain had lost her comparative advantage.

argued that, in practice, any cut in money wages would result in a corresponding fall in product prices, leaving the real wage unchanged and the labour market unaffected. Keynes and his followers also argued that a policy of wage cuts would be undesirable, because of its adverse effect on expectations and uncertainty. A continuous fall in wages and prices would depress business expectations, resulting in a decline in private investment and an increase in liquidity preference. Furthermore, Keynes argued that a policy of engineered wage cuts would threaten the very social fabric. In his lecture to the Harris Foundation in Chicago in 1931, he stated:

> 'Will not the social resistance to a drastic downward readjustment of salaries and wages be an ugly and dangerous thing? I am told sometimes that these changes present comparatively little difficulty in a country such as the United States where economic rigidity has not yet set in. I find it difficult to believe this. But it is for you, not me, to say. I know that in my own country a really large cut of money wages, a cut at all of the same order of magnitude as the fall in wholesale prices, is simply an impossibility. To attempt it would be to shake the social order to its foundation.' (Keynes, 1931, p. 31.)

Consequent to such thinking, Keynes suggested in his memorandum to the US Committee of Economic Advisers that it would be better to reduce real wages through a rise in prices either through a reflationary policy or by the imposition of a tariff, rather than by cutting nominal wages. According to Keynes, a rise in the price level would spread the burden of adjustment over a wider class of economic agents than would a cut in nominal wages, thereby minimising the chance of social unrest. Similarly, a 10 per cent uniform tariff would act immediately to produce a devaluation, lowering the equilibrium terms of trade, raising the price level, and reducing real wages.[1]

---

[1] In this regard, Keynes's policy prescriptions were not unique. Pigou, in his recommendations to the Macmillan Committee, advocated temporary reflationary policies and expansions in the money supply. Such policy recommendations are consistent with the Classical view of the source of wage rigidity, in that higher prices in the face of a given nominal level of benefits, for example, would also serve to reduce unemployment. In fact, some would argue that this is exactly what happened in Britain during the Second World War, when increases in the price level far exceeded the rise in nominal benefits (see Benjamin and Kochin, 1982).

Although the Classical and Keynesian explanations for high unemployment co-existed (albeit uneasily) through the twenties, the latter took the upper hand as the thirties progressed. We would suggest two independent but non-competing explanations for this development. First, there was the apparent posited mode of action of the Classical explanation. As we noted earlier, the behaviour of trade unions was frequently closely linked to the process of translating high unemployment benefits into wage rigidity and thus high unemployment.[1]

The second reason we would suggest for the demise of the Classical explanation lies in the world-wide spread of prolonged high unemployment during the thirties. How could the British unemployment insurance system (or its unions or trade boards) explain the emergence of debilitating unemployment in America? The answer, of course, is that it could not. This conclusion, combined with the perceived defects in the arguments espoused by Rueff, Pigou, Cannan and others, led observers to look elsewhere for explanations of the world-wide spread of unemployment. Keynes's *General Theory* seemed to be just the ticket, offering both diagnosis—deficient aggregate demand—and remedy—deficit spending. And once this approach was adopted, the insurance system disappeared from view in discussions of the unemployment problem.

3. The State of Play

The long-dormant Classical view of the inter-war years received a sharp stimulus with the publication of a series of provocative articles by Benjamin and Kochin (1978, 1979a, 1979b). The result has been a growing research programme focussing on inter-war unemployment. The evidence presented by Benjamin and Kochin begins with the hypothesis that the unemployment rate depends on

(i) the attractiveness of being unemployed, represented by un-

[1] The Classical explanation, as evidenced in the writings of Cannan and Churchill (cited above), freely acknowledges the impact of the insurance system on unemployment in non-union sectors. In the parlance of regression analysis, if the unemployment is the dependent variable, the co-efficient of unemployment benefits could be positive and statistically significant, even though the co-efficient on the interaction between benefits and unionisation is not significantly different from zero.

employment benefits relative to wages, sometimes referred to as the 'replacement rate'; and

(ii) the state of the economy relative to steady-state conditions, represented by the deviation of real GDP from trend.

In this framework, unemployment is made up of two components: 'cyclical unemployment' and the 'natural rate' of unemployment. Cyclical unemployment (that caused by changes in aggregate demand) depends on deviations of real GDP from its steady-state level, while the 'natural rate' of unemployment is given by the effects of the replacement rate. Benjamin and Kochin estimate that the inter-war unemployment insurance system raised the average unemployment rate by five to eight percentage points, and come to this provocative conclusion:

> 'The army of the unemployed standing watch at the publication of the *General Theory* was largely a volunteer army' (Benjamin and Kochin, 1979a).

Arguably, such rhetoric was meant to provoke as much as to stimulate, and it was not long before the 'establishment' replied. Adversarial criticism initially focussed on three main issues.[1] First, reservations were expressed about the quality and use of the data. It was argued that the use of benefits payable to a particular type of economic agent (a married man with two dependent children) was not representative, and could overstate the replacement rate.[2] Second, it was noted that the strong relationship between unemployment and the replacement rate may have been caused by officials who were adjusting the level of benefits in response to changes in the unemployment rate.[3] Third, it was claimed that the statistical significance of the replacement rate was sensitive to specification and sample size.[4]

---

[1] The brief discussion that follows does not pretend to do even modest justice to the 25 pages of criticisms levelled by four sets of authors in the April 1982 *Journal of Political Economy*, nor the 25 pages of reply by Benjamin and Kochin in that same issue. The interested reader is referred to the original papers (Cross, 1982, Collins, 1982, Ormerod and Worswick, 1982, and Metcalf *et al.*, 1982).

[2] Hatton (1980).

[3] See Casson (1983), p. 161, and Cross (1982).

[4] See Ormerod and Worswick (1982).

These criticisms were addressed by Benjamin and Kochin (1982) in a reply to their critics, in which they showed that:

(i) any sensible measure of inter-war unemployment benefits produces substantively identical results;

(ii) there is no credible evidence that political responses to unemployment were responsible for the observed association between benefits and unemployment; and

(iii) the appearance of non-robust statistical results vanishes once standard statistical criteria are applied.

Nevertheless, even critics sympathetic to the findings of Benjamin and Kochin have raised objections to the functional form of their estimating equation. Since unemployment and output are jointly determined in the macro-economy, the Benjamin and Kochin equation is not a true *reduced form.*[1] And since it incorporates both demand and supply factors, it cannot be considered a *structural equation* either.[2] Subsequent investigations into the issues raised by Benjamin and Kochin have attempted to avoid the problems potentially associated with this deficiency in their approach, by estimating alternative *structural models* of the labour market.[3]

(a) Time-Series Evidence

The first piece of evidence presented by Benjamin and Kochin consists of a time-series estimate of an equation of the form discussed above, and much of the subsequent work on the inter-war period has focussed on time-series data. Given the brevity of the inter-war period, it is unlikely that the time-series data contain enough information to permit robust discrimination

[1] A *reduced form* is the expression of a current endogenous variable (a variable to be explained) in terms of predetermined variables (variables that do the explaining).

[2] A *structural equation* represents a theoretical or behavioural hypothesis about a variable that is to be explained.

[3] Even a *structural model*, although more informative than a reduced form or quasi-reduced form, would still be only a partial analysis. The system would have to take as given the rest of the macro-economy. Thus a complete picture can be obtained only by estimating a full structural macro-economic model, as in Matthews (1986a).

among alternative structural models of the period. Nevertheless, this fact has not stopped researchers from using time-series data, chiefly (one imagines) because time-series data are so much easier to obtain. Two types of *quasi-structural models* have been estimated.[1] The *disequilibrium model*, associated with Keynesian views, assumes that markets fail to adjust in response to shocks. The *equilibrium model*, associated with Classical thinking, assumes that markets either clear continuously or clear subject to adjustment costs.

Both the equilibrium (Classical) and output-constrained (Keynesian) specifications were investigated by Hatton (1983). The novelty of Hatton's approach is his assumption that the replacement rate is a determinant of the demand for labour. His reasoning is that a rise in unemployment benefits induced a substitution towards temporary lay-offs in place of labour hoarding by employers, causing a reduction in labour demand without a commensurate contraction in production. Hatton finds that the insurance system produced a substantial increase in unemployment in inter-war Britain, although his interpretation of this result differs markedly from that of Benjamin and Kochin: Hatton argues that the causation comes from the demand side in a situation of general excess supply. Hatton concludes that his Keynesian specification is slightly preferable to his Classical specification, although neither specification performs very well. The Keynesian version, for example, 'produces parameter estimates inconsistent with a downward-sloping demand for labour' and yields a vertical labour supply curve. Overall, Hatton's specifications of the Keynesian and Classical models do not meet accepted theoretical norms; as a result, one might well conclude that, because of mis-specification by Hatton, there exists an alternative, superior specification. Such a specification is revealed in Chapter 5.

A Structural Disequilibrium Model

Broadberry (1983) has suggested a structural model of disequilibrium for the inter-war years, in which observed employment is given by labour demand (see Box 2, Figure B.2.1, below, pp. 90-91).

[1] We refer to them as *quasi-structural* because typically they are based only partially on utility or profit maximisation.

The problem with this approach is that excess supply in the aggregate labour market is incompatible with the fact that positive vacancies were observed during the inter-war years. Broadberry deals with this problem by asserting that some individual markets exhibited excess demand while others exhibited excess supply. Thus, aggregation gives total labour demand as employment plus vacancies and total supply as employment plus unemployment. This method side-steps the problem of separating observations of employment into excess supply or excess demand régimes. Broadberry's econometric results suggest that aggregate labour supply was totally inelastic in relation to the real wage and that labour demand was dominated by output demand considerations. Supposedly, benefits have no effect on labour supply decisions.

A major problem for Broadberry and for those who take the disequilibrium route is that there is no explanation for the disequilibrium and why it should persist. It fails to explain why the conventional forces of supply and demand failed to adjust the labour market. As will be seen in Chapter 5, an equilibrium approach which allows for labour market adjustment explains the period satisfactorily and is consistent with the wider body of theory accepted as conventional economics.

Irish and Winter (1981) and Smyth (1983) explicitly separate out employment observations as lying either on the demand curve or on the supply curve, as shown in Box 2, Figure 1. Smyth specifies an effective supply function which depends on the real wage and the replacement rate. The demand for labour depends on the product real wage, output and a quadratic time trend. Smyth postulates a nominal wage adjustment equation which implicitly assumes the existence of money illusion, because it ignores what is happening to prices. However, a re-specification of the model by Holden and Peel (1986) in terms of the real wage rather than the nominal wage makes little difference to the central conclusion: unemployment benefits were an important determinant of the inter-war supply of labour. Indeed, the Smyth-Holden-Peel results suggest that the insurance system raised inter-war unemployment on average by five to eight percentage points—a conclusion remarkably similar to that found by Benjamin and Kochin. Smyth argues that his results reject a market-clearing specification of the inter-war labour market, but

BOX 2

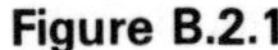

The Disequilibrium Model

Broadberry's specification was that the observed level of employment was always constrained by the short side of the market. This means that labour is rationed by demand when real wages are above equilibrium (W/P)* and rationed by supply when it is below (W/P). The implication is that actual employment is constrained to lie in the shaded area of Figure B.2:1. In

Figure B.2.1

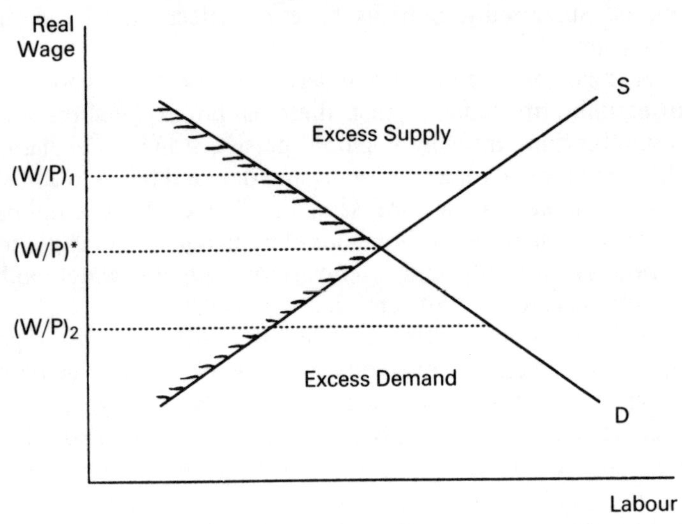

this conclusion is hardly decisive: there are simply too few observations to conduct robust hypothesis testing. All that can be said is that the data are not inconsistent with the view that the labour market failed to clear in the inter-war period. As with Hatton and Broadberry, Smyth found that the real wage contributed almost nothing to the explanation of labour supply.

Irish and Winter (1981), by contrast, find a statistically significant positive effect of wages on the supply of labour. However, their estimates, like those of many other investigators relying solely on time-series data, are seriously weakened by the

Figure B.2.2

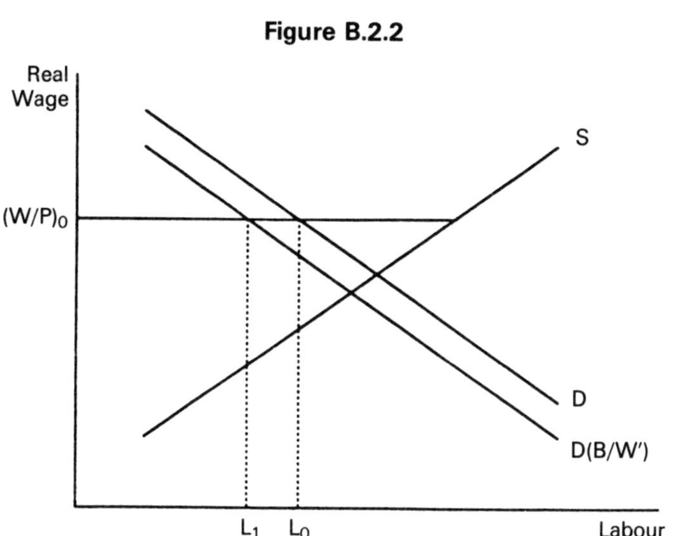

the inter-war period the situation would have been one of excess supply rather than excess demand.

The Hatton model assumes that the replacement rate affects the demand for labour negatively. A rise in the benefit-wage ratio enables firms to switch out of labour hoarding and in to short-time. Thus an increase in the replacement rate reduces the demand for labour (DD shifts down to the left in Figure B.2:2 above).

fact that there are simply too few time-series observations to make strong statistical inferences. Their tests on the wage-setting equation, for example, led to the conclusion that the data could support either the market-clearing or the non-market-clearing view, depending on which view was treated as the maintained hypothesis. This is a significant result, for it amounts to the conclusion that, given the amount of time-series data available for the inter-war period, statistical testing is unlikely to be able to differentiate between alternative models in terms of explanatory power. Thus, statistical testing has to be backed by both strong theory and plausible argument. In fact, the argument should be put in reverse order. Strong theory, historical observation and plausible explanation have to be backed by statistical analysis. At the end of the day it is the combination of all these elements that eventually persuades, not any single element alone.[1]

Structural Models of the Labour Market

More recent time-series research on the inter-war period has concentrated on fully structural models of the labour market. Beenstock and Warburton (1986a) estimate both labour demand and supply functions for the inter-war period and argue that unemployment benefits had no significant impact on unemployment. Despite the fact that Beenstock and Warburton offer no sound explanation for labour supply or the determination of real wages, they conclude that real wages and world trade growth were jointly responsible for the inter-war slump and subsequent recovery. What this amounts to saying is that real wages during the inter-war period were, for some unknown reason, too high—a conclusion that adds little to the debate.

In a later paper, Beenstock and Warburton (1986b) attempt to remedy this deficiency by estimating a wage adjustment function which assumes that real wages move in response to the deviation of the actual rate of unemployment from its natural rate. In principle, this model takes an intermediate position between the classical market-clearing model and the Keynesian disequilibrium model. The model consists of a labour demand schedule, a labour supply schedule and a wage adjustment equation. Box 3, Figure B.3.1 (below, p. 93) demonstrates the operation of the model. Labour supply, modelled as the participation rate, reacts positively to the real wage but negatively to the unemployment rate. The wage adjustment function reacts negatively to the rate of unemployment but positively to the level of real benefits. A fall in the demand for labour, caused by a demand shock, increases the registered level of unemployment, but a rise in the level of unemployment benefits increases wages (reduces effective labour supply) and also increases unemployment.

---

[1] Irish and Winter find that the implied rate of unemployment which had the market fully cleared was in the order of 13 per cent. This is similar to the natural rate of unemployment estimated by Matthews (1986a) using a full equilibrium macro-economic model for the period.

BOX 3

An Equilibrium Model

The Beenstock and Warburton model distinguishes between labour supply (the participation rate) and effective labour supply, which is given by the wage adjustment function.

The DD curve in Figure B.3:1 describes labour demand, the SS curve describes labour supply, and the WW curve describes the wage adjustment equation or effective labour supply. The gap between effective labour supply and potential labour supply as described by the participation rate at the real wage (W/P)* is the natural rate of unemployment (AB). A rise in benefits, other things equal, raises WW to the left, increasing the natural rate to, say, A′B′, while a rise in labour demand shifts the DD schedule up to the right, reducing the natural rate.

Figure B.3.1

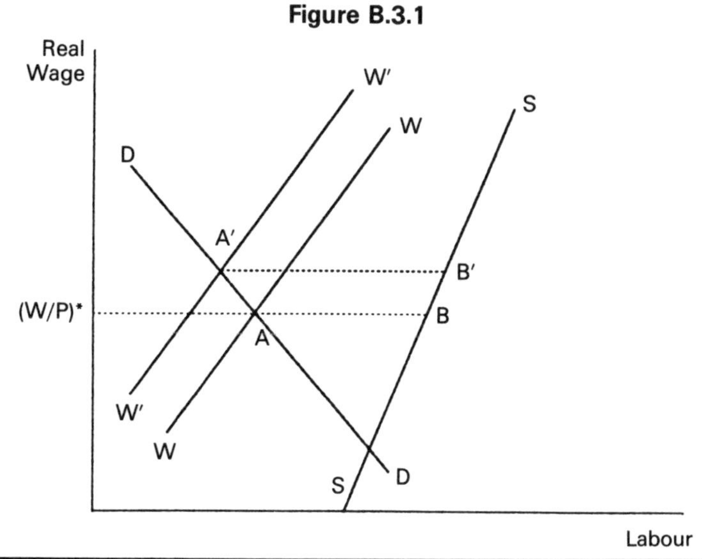

A fundamental problem with the Beenstock and Warburton model is that their wage-adjustment equation implies the existence of money illusion on the part of workers; a 1 per cent rise in prices would lead to a rise in nominal wages of only 0·26 per cent. Equivalently, their estimates imply that the act of adding a zero to all nominal values in the economy would convince workers that their real wages had risen, and thus cause a change in the natural rate of unemployment.

Hatton (1988) attempted to improve on the Beenstock and Warburton results by estimating a version of their model using quarterly data. Although he found that unemployment benefits positively influenced both the labour force participation rate and the level of wages, his wage-adjustment equation once again implies the existence of money illusion. Without an accompanying revision of the entirety of utility maximisation theory, it is difficult to take such estimates seriously.

Overall, though not uniformly, time-series research on the inter-war UK labour market supports the view of Benjamin and Kochin that both aggregate demand and unemployment insurance were important determinants of the prolonged high unemployment of the period. Recent work also suggests that it was nominal wages rather than real wages which exhibited rigidity during the period, and that a strictly Classical view of the world cannot fully account for the high unemployment of the period.[1] In assessing the usefulness of the time-series results, it is important to recognise a point emphasised repeatedly by Benjamin and Kochin (1979a, 1982): one of the problems associated with the use of time-series in examining the inter-war period is its brevity. Using annual data leaves a researcher with at most 19 observations. Quarterly data is available from 1924, but only for a few variables; other important variables have to be interpolated. Yet interpolation robs the data of its temporal independence, resulting in test statistics that are highly suspect. This implies that time-series data are unlikely to enable one to discriminate finely between competing hypotheses. It follows that any results based on time-series data must be evaluated in conjunction with cross-sectional evidence. It is to such evidence that we now turn.

(b) Cross-Sectional Evidence

In their original papers (1978, 1979a,b) and their reply to critics (1982), Benjamin and Kochin present a broad spectrum of cross-

[1] See Matthews (1987) for evidence of money wage rigidity in a Neo-Classical framework, but for an alternative interpretation see Broadberry (1986).

sectional evidence. Their first body of evidence concerns the unemployment record of juveniles (aged 16-17). During 1924-35, the years for which separate data on this group are available, the cyclical pattern of juvenile unemployment followed much the same course as that of the aggregate unemployment rate. However, juvenile unemployment averaged 5·0 per cent while aggregate unemployment averaged 14·6 per cent. Three possible explanations for this dramatic difference in unemployment experience were examined:

(i) systematic undercounting of juvenile unemployment;

(ii) over-representation of juveniles in trades that had abnormally low unemployment rates;

(iii) insulation of juveniles from the operation of the insurance system, due to low or non-existent benefits for this group.

The first explanation—systematic undercounting of juvenile unemployment—is refuted by the 1931 census, which emphatically corroborates the monthly insurance figures reported by the Ministry of Labour. There is some evidence supporting the second explanation, in that juveniles tended to be concentrated in low-unemployment industries, such as the distributive trades. However, there were no industries that employed an appreciable number of juveniles that had unemployment rates as low as the aggregate unemployment rate for juveniles. This and other factors lead Benjamin and Kochin to conclude that occupational choice can account for only a small part of the low unemployment rate among juveniles.

It is the third explanation—that the unemployment insurance system made unemployment an unattractive alternative to employment for juveniles—that Benjamin and Kochin find to be the most compelling explanation for low inter-war juvenile unemployment. Unemployment benefits available to single juveniles averaged only about 6·5 shillings a week. At age 18, the weekly level of benefits more than doubled, and at age 21 there was a further 50 per cent increase. Since these benefit increases for older persons far outstripped the wage increases they enjoyed, benefits relative to wages rose sharply at ages 18 and 21. This was compounded by the fact that people aged 18-20 who were in receipt of benefits for their dependants were able to receive the higher benefits otherwise available only to people over 21.

Importantly, not only was the benefit level low for juveniles, it was often the case that they were unable to collect any benefits. Between 20 and 30 weeks of insurance contributions were required before eligibility for benefits was established. Even though most people entered the work-force at ages 14 and 15, insurance coverage did not begin until age 16; thus, many juveniles (aged 16 and 17) were ineligible for the receipt of benefits when unemployed.

Unemployment Benefits Attractive to Older People

The pattern of unemployment observed during the inter-war years is strikingly consistent with the hypothesis that the insurance system induced high unemployment among older people, but not among juveniles. We noted above that benefits rose sharply relative to wages at age 18 and again at age 21.[1] Unemployment rates also rose sharply at age 18 and again at age 21. Moreover, although the ratio of unemployment benefits to wages is an important determinant of year-to-year movements in the *aggregate* unemployment rate, it does not help in explaining year-to-year movements in the *juvenile* unemployment rate.[2] Perhaps most importantly, the Benjamin and Kochin explanation of low inter-war juvenile unemployment yields several predictions that are strikingly confirmed by the evidence:

- The hypothesis implies that during the immediate post-war years (1948-66), when unemployment benefits were relatively low for all, unemployment among adults should have been lower relative to unemployment among juveniles than during the inter-war years. It was.
- The hypothesis implies that after 1966, when benefits for adults were raised relative to benefits for juveniles, the adult unemployment rate should have risen relative to the juvenile unemployment rate. It did.
- The hypothesis implies that when the school-leaving age was raised to 16 in 1972, making juveniles eligible for Supplementary Benefits during their first summer out of school, the juvenile unemployment rate should have risen relative to the adult rate. It did.

---

[1] Benjamin and Kochin (1979a, 1979b).

[2] *Ibid.*

- The hypothesis implies that when the government responded by ruling juveniles ineligible for benefits during their first summer out of school if they remained in school after Easter, the proportion of young people taking GCE/CSE exams should have dropped, as those expecting to do poorly dropped out of school to gain summer eligibility for benefits. It did.

The second body of cross-sectional evidence presented by Benjamin and Kochin concerns the impact on unemployment of the 1931 Anomalies Regulations. Until 1931, the unemployment rates for single and married women were on average almost exactly the same. After 1931, the unemployment rate among married women fell sharply relative to the rate among single women. In addition, unemployment among women as a whole fell markedly relative to unemployment among men after 1931. Both of these changes—quite pronounced even in the raw data—appear to have been caused by the unemployment insurance system.

As we noted in Chapter 3, it was commonplace for employers in the inter-war period either to refuse to hire married women or to discharge a woman upon marriage. After serving the standard waiting period, a married woman without work as a result of these practices was eligible for unemployment benefits—even if she quit voluntarily in anticipation of the application of the practice. Prompted in part by a belief that married women were exploiting the insurance system, the Anomalies Regulations, implemented in October 1931, substantially increased contributory requirements for married women, thereby making it much more difficult for them to qualify for unemployment benefits. The effects were immediate: tens of thousands of married women were disallowed benefits, unemployment among married women dropped sharply relative to unemployment among single women, and while male unemployment rose from 21·0 per cent in 1931 to 25·4 per cent in 1932, female unemployment fell from 18·0 to 13·6 per cent. Even after accounting for other factors influencing the unemployment rate, Benjamin and Kochin conclude that the Anomalies Regulations substantially reduced measured unemployment among women.

Nevertheless, the evidence on the Anomalies Regulations provides striking confirmation of the contention that no discussion of unemployment in inter-war Britain can hope to make sense without an explicit analysis of the effects of the insurance system.

Impact of Unemployment Insurance on Different Industries

The final body of cross-sectional evidence brought to bear by Benjamin and Kochin (1982) concerns the impact of the insurance system on individual industries. Examining seven industries for which the requisite data is available, they find that in all except one, the level of benefits relative to wages had a significant positive effect on unemployment during the inter-war years. The only industry to exhibit no statistically significant effect of benefits was electrical engineering—a high-wage, high-growth industry. Matthews (1986a) has extended these results for a broader sample of industries, using somewhat different techniques. He finds that, in general, the impact of the insurance system was to raise real wages, thereby reducing employment in the affected industries.

With the exception of Benjamin and Kochin's research, much of the work on inter-war unemployment thus far has focussed on time-series evidence. Recently, however, additional cross-sectional evidence has begun to emerge. Crafts (1987), for example, examines the impact of the insurance system on long-term unemployment in the thirties. He comes to four principal conclusions:

(i) although the statistical evidence indicates that the insurance system importantly affected the employment decisions of workers who had been unemployed continuously for three months or less, the system had but a minimal impact on those who had been continuously unemployed for more than 12 months;

(ii) an important reason for this result is that the long-term unemployed did 'not . . . [have] very high unemployment allowances relative to the wages they had normally earned';

(iii) instead, the rise in long-term unemployment in the 1930s was importantly due to 'duration dependency in re-employment probabilities'—in other words, the longer they remained unemployed, the harder it was to get re-employed; and

(iv) as a result, long-term unemployment was largely 'structural' and could not have been 'eliminated in the 1930s by modest reductions in the allowances payable or by a general expansion of aggregate demand'.[1]

Crafts attempts to examine the impact of the system on the unemployment of groups with different past unemployment rates by relating the unemployment rate of persons with prior continuous unemployment (less than three months; 12 months or more) to the economy-wide replacement rate and the current rate of bankruptcies (business failures). The latter variable is supposed to serve as a proxy for deviations of real GDP from trend, since this is not available on a quarterly basis, for this period. There is a critical problem with the use of current bankruptcies as a proxy. The rate of long-term unemployment is fundamentally a stock variable, reflecting the outcomes of current and past events. Similarly, the deviation of real GDP from trend represents the impact of current and past changes in aggregate demand: it measures the state of the economy relative to 'steady state', not the change in business conditions during the current quarter (or year). The current bankruptcy rate, however, is importantly a flow variable, useful in determining the change in the unemployment rate, rather than its level. Thus, equations of the form estimated by Crafts are conceptually mis-specified, and his conclusion that the system influenced the behaviour of the short-term unemployed but not that of the long-term unemployed may or may not be informative.

Just as importantly, even if a quarterly measure of the deviation of real GDP from trend (or its equivalent) could be devised, the estimated effect of the system on the unemployment decisions of the long-term unemployed will be approximately zero, even if the only reason they are unemployed is the insurance system. The reason for this is shown in Box 4, Figure B.4.2 (below, p. 101), which

[*Cont'd on p. 102*]

[1] Crafts (1987), pp. 430-31, where he also argues that job search by the long-term unemployed was minimal and that the high unemployment of the thirties had high welfare costs. Crafts presents no statistical evidence on search intensity, and the quotations from inter-war observers are equally consistent with the conclusion that the long-term unemployed had already obtained sufficient information about the labour market to know that they could not better themselves by giving up the dole. Hence they rationally chose not to devote any more resources to 'search' activity. For an expanded discussion of Crafts's paper, see Benjamin (1989).

BOX 4

The Micro Decision

Figure B.4:1 describes the distribution of wage incomes for all workers eligible for benefits in a hypothetical economy. The point A describes the level of flat-rate benefits. People whose wage income is below A are deemed to be in the so-called 'unemployment trap'—that is, they would be materially better off on the dole rather than in work. In terms of individual choice theory this situation is described in Figure B.4:2.

Figure B.4.1

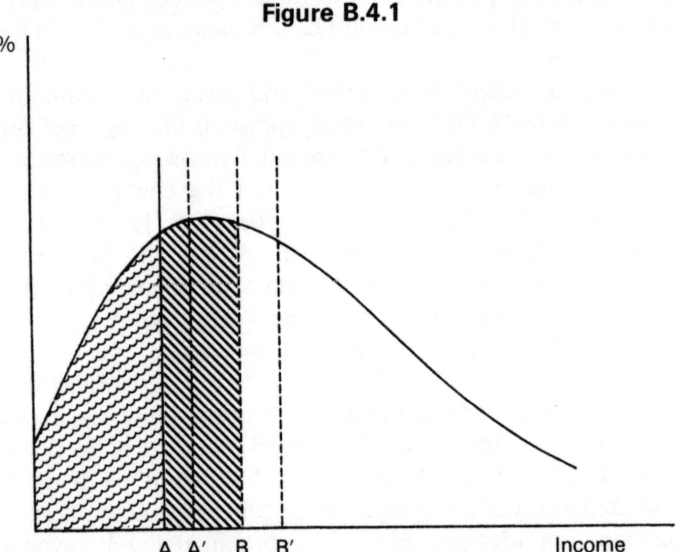

Figure B.4:2 describes the incentive framework for a person who is in the unemployment trap. The income-leisure trade-off is described by the line WL which measures the wage rate per unit of time available to the individual. The level of flat-rate benefit is given by OB. In the absence of benefits the individual would maximise his utility at the point P, receiving income OY and working HL units of time. It does not matter that people have to work a fixed number of hours in reality. It does not change the substance of the analysis—some adjustment is made through absenteeism.

OL is the maximum amount of leisure that can be consumed

Figure B.4.2

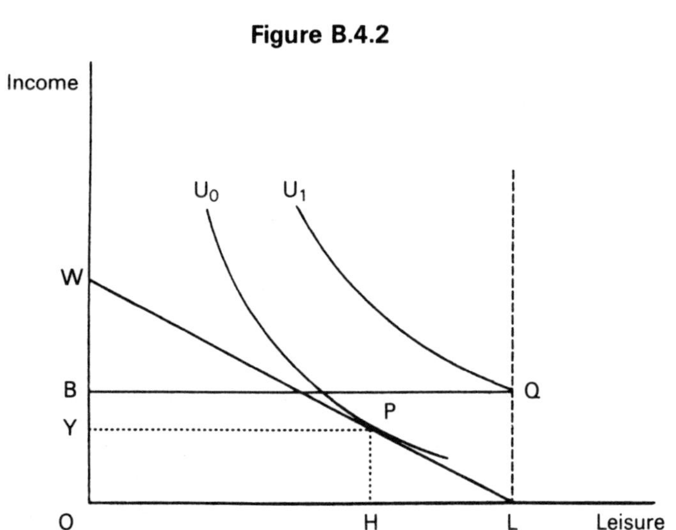

(say, 24 hours a day or seven days a week). If flat-rate benefits are introduced, it is clear that the individual is 'better off' obtaining OB rather than OY. Since benefits are independent of hours of work (leisure), the optimal point for the individual to be is at Q.

Figure B.4.3

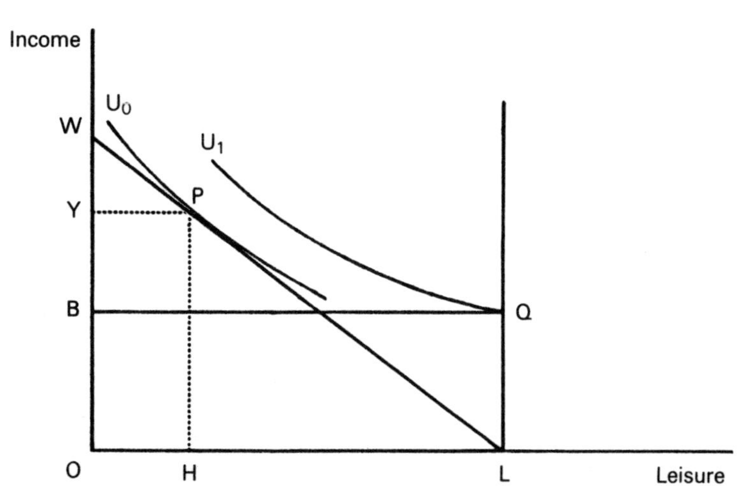

BOX 4 (continued)

The Micro Decision

Benefits do not only affect those in the unemployment trap. Even if a person is materially 'better off' in work than on the 'dole', in terms of individual welfare he may prefer to be on the dole rather than in work. This is because leisure has a premium. Individuals in this category would be those in the shaded area between A and B in Figure B.4:1. The optimal strategy of a person in this group is described by Figure B.4:3.

In this case, the wage income of the individual is OY which is greater than OB. However, because the value of leisure is positive (more than zero), the optimal point for the individual to be at is Q. Although the person is 'worse-off' in material terms, he is 'better-off' in terms of individual welfare.

Finally, the unshaded area in Figure B.4:1 is the position where earnings are sufficiently high so that flat-rate benefits do not affect the individual's optimal position.

Figure B.4.4

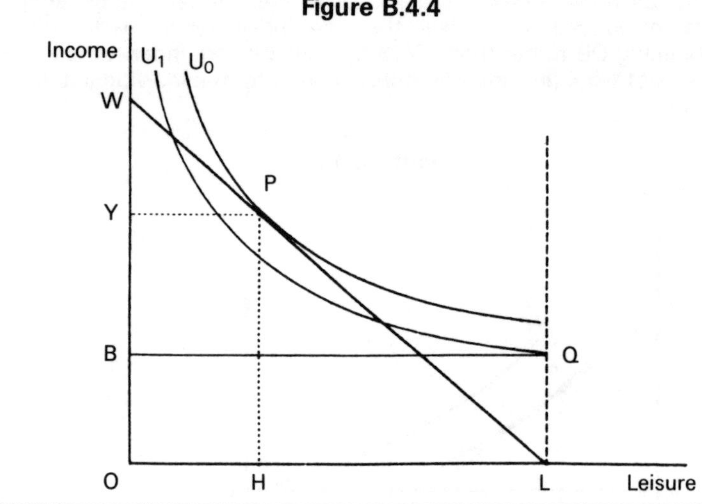

depicts an individual who is at a 'corner solution' at point Q, continuously unemployed at a replacement rate sufficiently high that 'modest reductions' in benefits relative to wages will not affect his behaviour. For such people, changes in the replacement rate are simply windfalls, and even 'correctly' estimated

Figure B.4.5

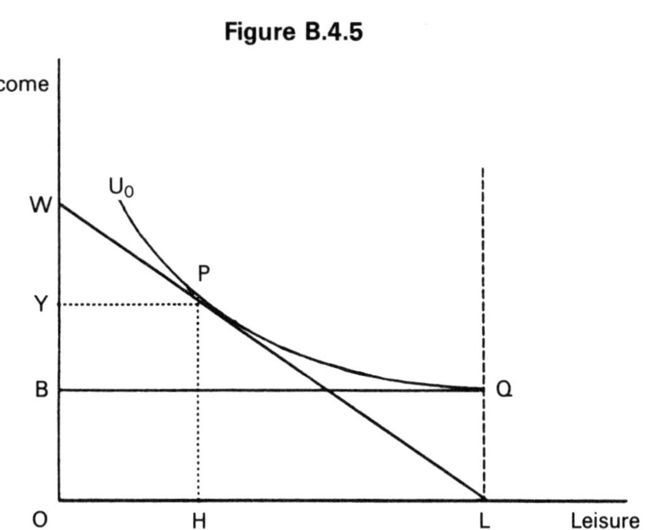

Figure B.4:4 illustrates this case. The wage facing the individual is given by the line WL and the wage income earned is OY. The optimal point for the individual is P, consuming OH units of leisure. If the person were to consume maximum leisure at benefits OB (point Q), he would clearly be worse off both in material and welfare terms.

What would be the effect of increasing the level of benefits? If the point A was moved to A′ in Figure B.4:1, this would not affect those who are already consuming the maximum amount of leisure, but it would draw more people into the shaded area to the right of the benefit level. A small increase in benefits will induce people on the margin to consume maximum leisure. This is illustrated in Figure B.4:5. At point P, the individual is indifferent between consuming OH leisure for OY income, and OL leisure for OB income. A small rise in benefits, other things equal, will increase individual welfare and induce maximum leisure consumption.

values of the coefficient of the replacement rate (B/W) will be (approximately) zero.[1]

[1] We say 'approximately' because there may be some people choosing [*Cont'd. on p. 104*]

Replacement Rates 'Too Low'?

Crafts's second contention—that replacement rates were somehow 'too low' to explain long-term unemployment because, for example, 'benefit to wage ratios for [men over 45] were only rarely over 80 per cent'—is most peculiar. We know of no 'magic' level for the replacement rate that will induce people to choose long-term unemployment, and doubt that Crafts does either. For some people, a replacement rate of 50 per cent may be sufficient; for others, a rate of 90 per cent might not be enough.[1] Beauty, after all, is in the eye of the beholder.

More generally, Crafts has missed two features of the labour market. *First*, estimates of earnings profiles show that wages follow a quadratic pattern over an individual's lifetime, rising to a peak at about age 50 and declining thereafter.[2] When combined with the fact that the interest rate is positive, this implies that the present value of an individual's future earnings peaks somewhat earlier and then begins declining quite drastically relative to current wages.[3] For a person deciding whether or not to be unemployed for a day, such forward-looking considerations are (largely) irrelevant: the relevant margin is today's benefits relative to today's wages. But for a person deciding about long-term unemployment, the relevant margin is the present value of benefits relative to the present value of wages. Given the pattern of lifetime earnings noted above, this implies that the ratio of current benefits to current wages will overstate the attractiveness of long-term unemployment for a person in his twenties or thirties, but it will understate the attractiveness of

---

continuous, long-term unemployment who are exactly at the margin. The rest of the long-term unemployed will be situated like the famous cartoon character, Andy Capp: willing to devote resources, if necessary, to make sure that they stay on the dole.

[1] One of the authors of this book maintains that, once his son graduates from college, 60 per cent would do quite nicely. The other author, perhaps because he is younger and faced with a penal mortgage, avers that he would continue working even at 90 per cent.

[2] See Mincer (1974).

[3] For example, under plausible assumptions, for an individual whose present value of future earnings at age 40 is 10 times as great as current earnings, when that person is 55, the present value of future earnings is only five times as great as current earnings. See Benjamin (1989) for a complete discussion.

long-term unemployment for a person in his forties, fifties or sixties.[1]

Secondly, computations of the replacement rates referred to by Crafts are based on 'normal' wages—which are actually the wages the person was earning when last employed. Yet human capital depreciates when an individual is out of work, implying that the wages available to a person who has been unemployed for a long period will be well below the wages available when he first became unemployed. Once again, the relevant replacement rate will be understated by the measured replacement rate, implying that the incentive to remain unemployed will be understated.[2]

Crafts's third point—that re-employment probabilities diminish as a function of unemployment duration—is surely correct. Yet he writes as though unemployment duration was somehow exogenous, and therefore to be treated as an independent variable. In fact, studies of the effects of unemployment benefits on unemployment duration uniformly find that higher benefits induce greater unemployment duration. We are not claiming that only benefits increase duration. Rather, we would argue that if one wants to understand the full effects of the inter-war system, one must recognise that it increased durations and thus reduced re-employment probabilities. Crafts argues that on the basis of contemporary reports, there was a significant amount of duration dependence—that is, the longer a person was unemployed the harder it became for him to be re-employed.

In the light of the foregoing, Crafts's conclusion that by the late 1930s, cuts in benefits and increases in aggregate demand would not appreciably have reduced the incidence of long-term unemployment, must be tempered in two dimensions. *First*, it

---

[1] For trades with relatively flat earnings profiles, this degree of distortion will be modest—perhaps as little as 10 per cent. But for 'young men's trades' such as coal-mining, the degree of understatement of the attractiveness of long-term unemployment can easily be 50 per cent or more. See Benjamin (1989) for further details.

[2] Moreover, as Crafts notes correctly, the operation of the benefits system influenced the response of the long-term unemployed to the labour market in even more subtle ways. The widespread reluctance of the long-term unemployed to accept casual work or lower-paid work was in part because it meant disqualification from benefits in the former case, and re-categorisation by the unemployment authorities as low-grade labour in the latter.

seems likely that much more long-term unemployment in the thirties was due to the insurance system than Crafts would have us believe. *Secondly*, even if by the late thirties, long-term unemployment could not have been cut appreciably by cutting benefits, the relevant counter-factual question is somewhat different: By how much would long-term unemployment have been lower in the late 1930s if benefits had been lower throughout the decade? To us, the answer seems inescapable: a great deal lower.

Evidence from London

In another recent study, Eichengreen (1987a) examines cross-section survey data of working-class London collected by the London School of Economics during 1929-31. The sample was taken from 27,000 case record cards completed in the course of the survey. For the entire sample, a small but positive association between the replacement rate and unemployment was found for adult males. When the sample is separated into sub-samples comprising household heads and other adult males, the additional detail is revealing. Among household heads, Eichengreen finds that the replacement rate had no statistically significant effect on the probability of unemployment; among other adult males, however, he finds the association to be large and statistically significant. Insight into the reasons for Eichengreen's results may be found in Tables 4 and 5. Table 4 presents the characteristics of the sample (taken from Eichengreen (1987a), Table 1). Note the striking differences in the age and earnings of household heads as against other adults: on average, household heads were in their early forties while other males were in their early twenties, and the earnings of household heads, even of those recently unemployed, were higher than the national average for that period, while the earnings of other males were significantly lower. As a result, replacement rates were lower for heads of households than for those who were not heads of households. Also, wage-rates in general were significantly higher in London than elsewhere, as shown in Table 5, which details the breakdown of earnings by region.

The pattern that emerges is exactly what one would expect under the insurance system hypothesis. Even though wages were much higher in London than elsewhere, the insurance authorities

TABLE 4

CHARACTERISTICS OF THE SAMPLE: LONDON SURVEY DATA, 1929-31
(adult males)

Males	All Adult Males			Household heads			Other		
Variable	All	Emp'd	Unemp'd	All	Emp'd	Unemp'd	All	Emp'd	Unemp'd
Age	38·2	38·2	38·0	42·6	42·6	43·1	23·4	23·4	23·1
% Ill	1·6	1·5	3·3	2·1	1·9	3·8	0·4	0·2	1·9
% Residing in own home	2·7	2·9	1·0	3·5	3·7	1·3	0·2	0·2	0·0
% working spouse	5·1	4·9	7·6	6·7	6·3	10·2	0·0	0·0	0·0
% unemployed spouse	0·2	0·1	0·5	0·2	0·2	0·6	0·0	0·0	0·0
Weekly earnings (S/-)	55·2	55·9	47·2	59·3	60·0	51·0	41·6	42·1	36·3
Non-wage Income (S/-)	4·3	4·1	6·6	4·0	3·7	7·2	5·1	5·2	4·7
Other Income* (S/-)	26·9	26·5	31·5	19·3	19·0	23·8	52·2	52·1	53·7
% Unemployed	8·6	0·0	100	8·3	0·0	100	9·6	0·0	100
Children	1·3	1·3	1·2	1·3	1·3	1·2	1·3	1·3	1·3
Number	2,440	2,230	210	1,879	1,723	156	561	507	54

*Other than wages and benefits of current worker only.

Source: B. Eichengreen, 'Unemployment in Inter-war Britain: Dole or Doldrums?', *Oxford Economic Papers*, Vol. 39, 1987.

TABLE 5

REGIONAL DISTRIBUTION OF EARNINGS BY INDUSTRY: UK, 1929
(*shillings/week*)

Region	Metal Ind.	Transport	Construction	Dist. Trades
London	72/6	63/6	69/4½	59/10
N. Counties	65/4½	55/9	61/10	59/2
Yorkshire	65/11	58/1	63/3	53/9
Lanc. & Chesh.	67/1	58/5	62/6	53/6
N. Midlands	64/9	55/-	63/4½	53/9
W. Midlands	66/6	65/-	62/8	49/8
S. Midlands	63/10	50/10	54/7	53/9
S. East	63/5	52/10	55/2	55/4
S. West	62/11	52/10	55/5	55/4
Wales	69/10	62/6	60/11	53/6
Scotland	65/8	54/5	64/10	52/11
N. Ireland	61/3½	61/7	65/-	n/a

Source: Unweighted averages of rates of wages of classes of worker within broad industry classification in Ministry of Labour, *Standard Time Rates of Wages and Hours of Labour in Great Britain and Northern Ireland* at 31 August 1929, London: HMSO, 1929.

did not pay a 'London premium'. As a result, the replacement rate in London was much lower than elsewhere, resulting in a smaller overall impact of the system there than elsewhere.[1] Within London itself, wages for heads of household were much higher than for non-heads of household. Thus, the former group had lower replacement rates and showed much smaller effects of the insurance system.

The existence of unemployment benefits also tends to explain another important cross-sectional feature of the inter-war period–the narrowing of skill differentials in wages. Casson (1983) examines the work of Rowe (1928), who found in his study of five industries that, between 1920 and 1926, the wage-rates of unskilled workers rose relative to the wage-rates of semi-skilled

[1] This result reminds us that it is dangerous to try to write British economic history based on what one observes in London.

TABLE 6

WAGES BY SKILL IN FIVE BRITISH INDUSTRIES
(1913 = 100)

Industry	Grade	Job	Wage Index 1920	Wage Index 1926
Building	Skilled	Bricklayer	94	104
	Semi-skilled	Painter	105	117
	Unskilled	Labourer	124	121
Coalmining	Skilled	Coal-getter	110	97
	Semi-skilled	Putter & filler	118	96
	Unskilled	Labourer	123	99
Cotton	Skilled	Mule spinner	118	106
	Semi-skilled	Grinder	123	110
	Unskilled	Woman weaver	125	112
Engineering	Skilled	Turner	97	93
	Semi-skilled	Machineman	109	98
	Unskilled	Labourer	120	105
Railways	Skilled	Engine driver	91	117
	Semi-skilled	Guard	104	123
	Unskilled	Goods porter	125	127

Source: Rowe (1928), Table III, p. 48, quoted in Casson (1982), p. 181.

and the wage-rates of semi-skilled workers rose relative to the wages of skilled workers—a finding reproduced in Table 6.

Casson suggests three possible explanations for these patterns: first, the behaviour of trade unions; second, the advance of technology; and third, the level of unemployment benefits. Casson rejects the first because it cannot explain the fact that the wages of unskilled women also showed a relative improvement during this period (see Routh, 1980, p. 124).

The second factor—technological advance—clearly shaped industrial histories in some pockets of industry—particularly the new industries such as motor vehicles, light engineering and services—but not in the old staples (in the main those examined by Rowe (1928)). To the extent that unskilled women were over-represented in the new industries, technological change may explain why their wages improved relative to the wages of unskilled men, but it fails to explain why the wages of unskilled men rose relative to the wages of semi-skilled and skilled men in the face of mass unemployment. Casson half-heartedly accepts the possibility that the insurance system may have played a rôle, but he dismisses it as a complete explanation, because unskilled women were poorly unionised.

What Casson fails to recognise is the very fact that we have emphasised earlier: the transmission mechanism from benefits to wages does not require trade unions. The relevant fact is that unemployment benefits for women without dependants were 80 per cent of those payable to similarly situated men between 1920 and 1924, while on average, women's wages were less than this—about 45 to 50 per cent lower than average male wages.[1] Similarly, since the insurance authorities did not pay skill differentials, replacement rates among men would tend to be negatively correlated with skill levels, implying a larger upward impact of the system on the wages of unskilled workers relative to the wages of skilled workers.

In summary, the cross-sectional evidence uncovered thus far reveals a pattern that is inescapable: the inter-war unemployment insurance system importantly shaped the unemployment histories of every nook and cranny of Britain. Whether one examines the pattern by age, sex, industry, duration, location or skill, one simple fact emerges: lowering the cost of an activity induces more of that activity. In the present instance, lowering the cost of unemployment induced more unemployment in inter-war Britain. We turn now to the experience of inter-war America.

4. The US Experience

The literature on the inter-war American labour market is less well developed than the literature on the inter-war British labour market, for two reasons. *First*, as noted earlier (above, pp. 26-27), the twenties were a halcyon period for the US economy, lacking the mystery of an unusually high unemployment rate to explain. *Second*, the high US unemployment of the thirties has generally been regarded as being easily explained by the Great Depression and its aftermath. Interest in the period has, however, been stimulated by the work of Darby (1976). In his paper, Darby argues that the apparent failure of the Lucas and Rapping (1972)

---

[1] Department of Employment and Productivity, *British Labour Statistics: Historical Abstract 1886-1968*, London: HMSO, 1971.

search-anticipations model to track unemployment during the 1930s was mainly due to inaccuracies in the measurement of unemployment and wages. In brief, the search-anticipations model states that deviations from the natural rate of unemployment occur as labour supply responds to deviations in wages and prices (W,P) from their anticipated values (W*,P*) where the anticipated wage and price levels are generated by an adaptive expectations schema, in which m is the expectations adjustment parameter.[1] The model states that unemployment deviates from its natural rate when wages or prices deviate from workers' anticipations.

The data used by Lucas and Rapping to estimate this model treated as unemployed those individuals who were participants in the federal relief programmes of the time, including those working on WPA-sponsored work projects. Darby argues that such people should not be treated as unemployed, but simply as being government employees. Table 7 presents the original unemployment data from Lebergott (1964) and the Bureau of Labor Statistics (BLS), together with adjustments for the number of relief workers. Treating people in receipt as being employed produces a marked drop in the measured unemployment rate of the thirties.

Even 'correcting' the unemployment figures for the number of people on relief, Darby was unable to produce a well-fitting model of the search-anticipations type. However, when this adjustment was combined with a new wage series, which measured the average annual earnings of full-time equivalent (FTE) employees, Darby concluded that the simple search-anticipations model could be used to explain the behaviour of unemployment in the USA during the thirties. Darby also concluded that the slow fall in unemployment from 1934 to 1941 'is shown to be a fiction based on erroneous data'. Although between 5 and 7 per cent of the labour force was employed in counter-cyclical public work programmes during 1934-40, he concludes there is no evidence that unemployment would have been higher in the absence of these programmes.

[1] Specifically, $W^*_t = mW_t + (1-m)(1+g_1)W_{t-1}$ and $P^*_t = mP_t + (1-m)(1+g_2)P_{t-1}$, where m is a weighting constant and g_1 and g_2 are trend growth rates in wages and prices respectively.

TABLE 7

US UNEMPLOYMENT RATES, 1929-41

Year	Lebergott	Bureau; Lebergott	Corrected Bureau	Corrected
1929	3·2	3·2	3·2	3·2
1930	8·9	8·7	8·9	8·7
1931	16·3	15·9	15·7	15·3
1932	24·1	23·6	22·9	22·5
1933	25·2	24·9	20·9	20·6
1934	22·0	21·7	16·2	16·0
1935	20·3	20·1	14·4	14·2
1936	17·0	16·9	10·0	9·9
1937	14·3	14·3	9·2	9·1
1938	19·1	19·0	12·5	12·5
1939	17·2	17·2	11·3	11·3
1940	14·6	14·6	9·5	9·5
1941	9·9	9·9	6·0	6·0

Source: Darby (1976).

Although Darby's work highlights the potential for an equilibrium interpretation of US unemployment in the 1930s, his results have been subjected to severe criticism. The coefficient of adjustment on the anticipated values of wages and prices is unusually low, producing an extremely slow correction of discrepancies between actual and anticipated wages and prices. This slow adjustment has been shown to be crucial to Darby's results[1] and does not conform well with more recent theories of rational expectations.[2] Furthermore, the search-anticipations model does not fit comfortably with the widespread evidence on the existence of long-term unemployment, and the Darby specification suffers from the same problem as the Benjamin and Kochin model for the UK: it is a quasi-reduced form. Thus, the

[1] Kesselman and Savin (1978).

[2] Broadberry (1982) finds that the Darby model collapses once re-estimated for rational expectations.

model cannot distinguish between shocks to the labour market from the demand side and shocks from the supply side. Finally, Darby simply asserts that people on relief would in fact have been employed in the private sector in the absence of the relief programmes.

In an exploratory paper on the effects of public relief, utilising cross-section data for 1935, Wallis and Benjamin (1981) found that the programmes were in fact drawing recipients from the ranks of the already unemployed, thereby leaving private sector employment unaffected. The implication is that, without the relief programmes, recipients would have been unemployed, so that the original method of treating them as unemployed was correct. The Wallis and Benjamin treatment has two advantages. First, the estimates are all based on an explicit structural model. Second, instead of merely asserting what individuals would have done in the absence of the relief programmes, they explicitly estimate the impact of the programmes on the private labour market. As they explicitly note, Wallis and Benjamin's results are subject to two major limitations: first, their data is cross-sectional only, and focuses only on the impact of FERA in the 53 cities for which data were then available; second, the model is estimated under the maintained hypothesis that relief authorities adjusted benefits on a regular basis so as exactly to clear the market for relief cases.

In a more recent study, Wallis and Benjamin (1986) have attempted to correct these deficiencies. The data base, for example, has been extended to cover the state-level operations of both FERA and the WPA programmes for the entire period of 1933-40. In addition, they have modified the specification of the model to allow for the possibility of rationing in the market for relief cases. Their preliminary results suggest that:

(i) there is significant evidence that applicants for relief were rationed by non-price means; and

(ii) although the FERA programme appears to have had a minimal impact on the private labour market, the WPA had a significant effect, albeit much smaller than that suggested by Darby.

5. Conclusions

Our assessment of the state of research on the inter-war labour market suggests three broad conclusions. First, the cross-sectional evidence on the UK labour market leaves little doubt that the inter-war system of unemployment insurance importantly shaped both the level and the nature of unemployment during the inter-war years. No commentary on this period in British history can hope to understand events without explicitly accounting for the effects of unemployment benefits.

Secondly, the time-series evidence on the British experience is broadly consistent with the cross-sectional results, and provides a tentative estimate that the insurance system raised the unemployment rate by five to eight percentage points—an estimate confirmed by the cross-sectional data.[1] The time-series evidence is, however, clouded by the limited amount of data and by a failure of existing structural models to incorporate certain Classical features suggested by the cross-sectional evidence.

Finally, the evidence on the US labour market during the thirties, while much more rudimentary, suggests that the relief programmes of this period must be considered in understanding the behaviour of unemployment. It is also clear, particularly in the light of the British experience, that cross-sectional evidence must be brought to bear if conclusive answers are to be reached. We turn now to an examination of the issues left unresolved thus far.

---

[1] See Benjamin and Kochin (1982).

5

TRUE GRIT

Introduction

THIS CHAPTER ARTICULATES our analytical model of the labour market in the USA and the UK. Our major focus in using the model will be to examine the effect of the 'dole' in the UK, and 'work relief' in the USA, on wages and unemployment. The question of concern is simple: What was the source of real wage rigidity during the inter-war period? This question has long puzzled both the historian and the economist. For example, Lucas and Rapping conclude that since the search-anticipations theory does not explain the source of real wage rigidity in the US inter-war labour market, the depression creates problems for any theory:

> 'Once one attempts to obtain a quantitative explanation for wage-price rigidity in terms of individual and market behaviour, there is no traditional theory to return to.' (Lucas and Rapping, 1972, p. 191.)

We develop a model that attempts to capture much of the analysis of the classical economists of the time. The model recognises that the quantity of labour demanded varies inversely with the real cost of labour, and that the supply of labour responds to classical incentives. The framework of analysis is in terms of equilibrium, and therefore takes up the challenge implicit in Lucas and Rapping (1972). The model concentrates on the supply side, a dimension largely ignored in contemporary macro-economic models, let alone in explanations of the inter-war period. We do not argue that the unemployment of the 1930s was entirely the result of supply-side factors. On the contrary, we find that the conventional view, in which unemployment was importantly the result of severe contractionary demand shocks, explains much of the history of the period. Nevertheless, in drawing from the analysis of the classical economists of the period (including Keynes), our model yields an explicit and empirically important 'rôle for the dole'. In doing so, it reveals in some detail the necessity for revising conventional views of the economic and social history of the inter-war era in both the USA and the UK.

1. The Model

A model is an analytical aid. It helps to reduce a complex world into a framework of analysis which cuts out the peripheries and focuses on fundamental issues. Global or literal explanation is not the aim of the construction of a model—a methodological impossibility in any event. Rather, the aim is to simplify. The power of a model is in its predictive ability. The more general a model, the more it should be able to explain as a special case of competing or alternative models. Furthermore, it should be able to explain (by prediction) phenomena that are strictly outside the confines of that which is to be explained. For example, it should be capable of explaining similar phenomena across differing institutional settings—such as, labour markets in different countries. Similarly, a more general model should be able to explain the same phenomena over different time-periods, such as post-war as well as inter-war. But it should always be borne in mind that a model is not a literal explanation. It is, as McClosky (1983) describes it, a metaphor—and the simpler the model, the greater the metaphor.

As a starting point, our model distinguishes between a unionised and a non-unionised labour market. The popular views of the labour markets in the USA and UK during the inter-war years typically portray the former as being fundamentally non-union and the latter as heavily unionised. As Table 8 indicates, such a portrayal contains elements of truth, but misses some important features. Both countries began the inter-war years with unionisation rates that were relatively high by their historical standards, and markedly higher in the UK than in the

TABLE 8

UNION DENSITY: UK AND USA, 1920-39

(*Union membership as a percentage of working population*)

Year	UK	USA
1920	40·4	17·5
1921	33·0	18·0
1922	28·4	13·8
1923	27·6	11·4
1924	28·0	11·2
1925	27·3	10·6
1926	25·6	10·3
1927	24·0	10·3
1928	23·2	10·1
1929	23·2	9·6
1930	22·5	11·6
1931	21·1	12·4
1932	20·1	12·9
1933	19·8	11·3
1934	20·6	11·9
1935	21·7	13·2
1936	23·3	13·7
1937	25·2	22·6
1938	25·7	27·5
1939	–	28·6

Source: H. Pelling (1973), *A History of British Trade Unionism*, Penguin Books, 2nd edn., pp. 280-82; and US Dept. of Commerce, *Historical Statistics of the United States: Colonial Times to the 1970s*, part I, pp. 126 and 178.

USA. And in both countries, union membership dropped sharply during the deflation of the early twenties. Modest declines in membership (as a fraction of the work-force) continued through the rest of the twenties, followed by relative stability during the first half of the thirties, with membership rates in the UK remaining roughly double those in the USA. Economic expansion during the later thirties brought growth in union membership in both countries, a process noticeably enhanced in the USA by the 1935 passage of the Wagner Act (discussed below, pp. 129-130). The result was that by the end of the inter-war period, the unionisation rate in the USA actually exceeded that in the UK.

On the demand side of the labour market, we assume that employment varies inversely with the real wage. In other words, demand curves slope downwards—hardly a controversial assumption.[1] Whether the economy is believed to be Keynesian demand-constrained, perfectly competitive or imperfectly competitive, the basic proposition that the quantity of labour demanded varies inversely with the real wage is something that must hold, given conventional assumptions about production technology and the behaviour of firms.

(a) The UK

The evidence for a downward-sloping demand curve for labour in the UK inter-war period is overwhelming. In a series of independent studies, Casson (1983), Beenstock and Warburton (1986a), Hatton (1988), Smyth (1983) and Matthews (1987) estimate downward-sloping demand schedules for labour for this period. Clearly, this part of the model is uncontroversial and would seem acceptable to all schools of thought.

It is on the supply side that the model departs from most modern treatments. At the outset, we distinguish explicitly between union and non-union sectors. We assume that unions set the wage-rate so as to maximise the representative member's utility, subject to the demand for union labour. Thus, the union sets the wage and the employer (of union labour) decides on the level of employment. The mechanics of this optimising exercise need not detain us here and can be found in Oswald (1982); the essential point to note is that the union wage is set as a 'mark-up' on the non-union wage.

The non-union sector is assumed to be fully competitive, and the market for non-union labour is assumed to clear continuously—in the sense that, given expectations and non-work alternatives, those non-union workers willing to work are able to do so. The supply of labour to the non-union sector

[1] Although a surprisingly large amount of empirical work in the UK is based on a rejection of precisely such a view. Up until recently, few of the major UK Keynesian-type macro-economic models (including the Treasury model) allowed for a direct effect of real wages on employment.

depends on demographic factors and the replacement rate—that is, unemployment benefits relative to wages. The level of real unemployment benefits defines a 'floor' for the non-union wage-rate; that is, we assume that real wages in the non-union sector do not fall below the point defined by the level of real benefits. Figure B.5:1 in Box 5 demonstrates the effect of a rise in the level of benefits on wages and employment.

Three problems remain. *First*, our theory distinguishes between the union and non-union sectors, when aggregate data on wages and employment generally do not. This problem is solved by simply aggregating the two sectors to obtain an aggregate wage-setting function. *Second*, we must take into account that unions do not bargain for real wages, but for money wages based on some expectation of the price level over the contract period. This means that over the contract period, the real wage will vary negatively with unexpected inflation. Therefore, the specification of labour supply must allow for unexpected changes in the price level. *Third*, it turns out that the union maximisation exercise produces a 'mark-up' on the non-union wage, which depends on the elasticity of demand for labour. The problem is that this elasticity could vary from industry to industry and also by the degree of unionisation. This last problem is solved by assuming that the elasticity of demand for labour varies negatively with unionisation. That is to say, the lower the elasticity of demand for labour, the higher the unionisation rate, and consequently the higher the 'mark-up'. This assumption is predicated on our belief that it is no accident that union density is greater in those industries where the demand for labour is relatively inelastic. It makes sense for unions to organise where they are able to exploit monopoly power.

Given these assumptions, the wage-setting function (the labour supply curve) relates real wages positively to union density, the real value of benefits, and employment, and negatively to unemployment and to unanticipated changes in the price level. The full structure of the model is outlined in Box 5. Briefly, a rise in real benefits raises the real wage in the non-union sector, as individuals substitute out of work and into leisure. Given the union 'mark-up' over the non-union wage, this raises the target real wage for the union sector. Ultimately, the

BOX 5

The Labour Sector Model

The effect of a change in benefits is illustrated in Figure B.5:1.

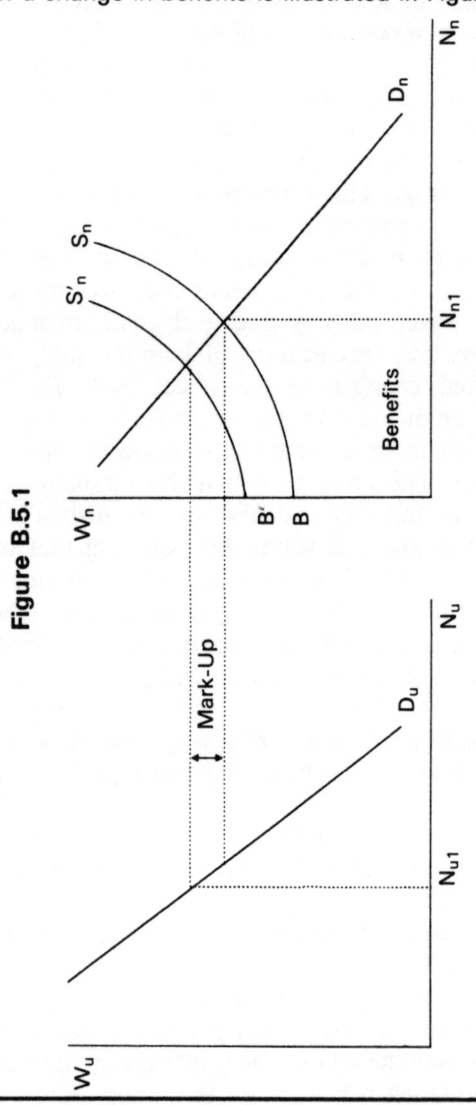

Figure B.5.1

The supply of labour in the non-union sector depends on the real wage in the non-union sector and the level of real benefits, which acts as a floor to the real wage. The supply curve is drawn flat (asymptotic) to the benefit level because at high replacement rates, labour supply would be expected to have a higher elasticity than at low replacement rates. A rise in the level of benefits causes a shift of S_n up to the left, raising the real wage in the non-union sector. Given the union mark-up decision, this also raises the real wage in the union sector. Labour displaced in the union sector will bid down the wage in the non-union sector and moderate the initial rise in the non-union wage. These second-round effects can best be understood by aggregating the two sectors.

The total demand for labour is made up of the demand for labour in the union sector, D_u, and the demand for labour in the non-union sector, D_n. So

$$D = D_u\ (w_u,\ k) + D_n\ (w_n,\ k) \qquad (1)$$

where k is a vector of shift variables. From Figure B.5:1 we note that the union wage is given as a 'mark-up' on the non-union wage. As a simplification, assume that this mark-up is fixed. Then (1) can be written as

$$D = D(m,\ k,\ w_n)$$

where m is the 'mark-up'.

Since the wage in the union sector is given by the wage in the

Figure B.5.2

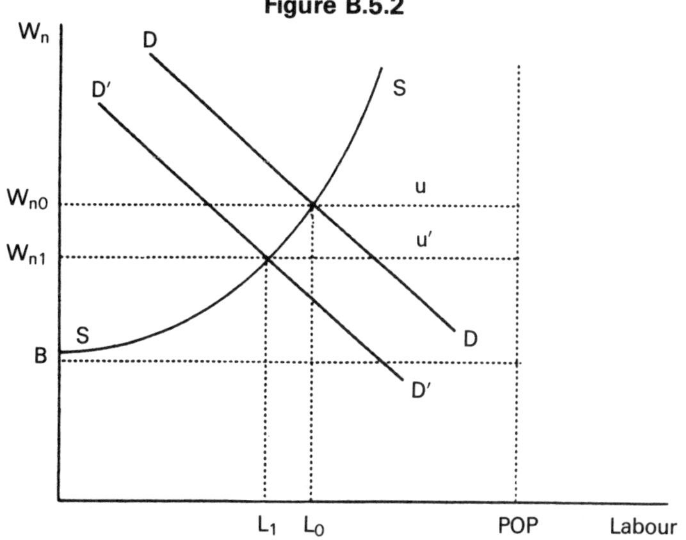

BOX 5 (continued)

The Labour Sector Model

non-union sector, we can examine the effects of the full model by operating on the wage in the non-union sector.

A rise in the 'mark-up' caused by a rise in the union rate, shifts the aggregate demand for labour in terms of the non-union wage-rate down to D'D' (in Figure B.5:2), pushing down the wage in the non-union sector and raising the equilibrium level of unemployment from u to u'.

A rise in the real value of benefits (from, say, B to B') causes a shift in the supply schedule SS up to S'S' in Figure B.5:3 (see also Minford *et al.*, 1985), raising the non-union wage and increasing equilibrium unemployment from u to u'.

Other factors that will cause a shift in the DD schedule include the effect of a rise in demand for UK exports (rise in world trade), which pushes UK export prices above foreign prices, as firms move up their marginal cost curves, and raises the real exchange rate. This increases the demand for labour as firms extend their margin of production.

During the inter-war period in the UK, the rate of unionisation fell in the early 1920s, shifting DD up to the right (i.e., increasing the demand for labour), but real benefits also rose dramatically, shifting SS up to the left (i.e., reducing the supply of labour). In

impact is a decline in employment, and a rise in unemployment, in both the union and non-union sectors.[1]

The Mechanism Established

By now the mechanism by which benefits affect wages and unemployment should be clear. As Figure B.5:1 in Box 5 indicates, a rise in benefits reduces labour supply in the non-

[1] In the context of the UK inter-war period, for example, it was the fall in prices combined with the continuous rise in benefits that raised real benefits by over 125 per cent between 1921 and 1938: the fall in money wages that followed the sharp fall in prices was less than proportional. Unions were able to resist one-for-one reductions in wages with the fall in prices because the rising real level of benefits raised the floor to real wages. Thus, we shall argue, unemployment benefits provide the key to understanding the so-called 'wage rigidity factor' that bedevilled Keynesian explanations of the inter-war period.

Figure B.5.3

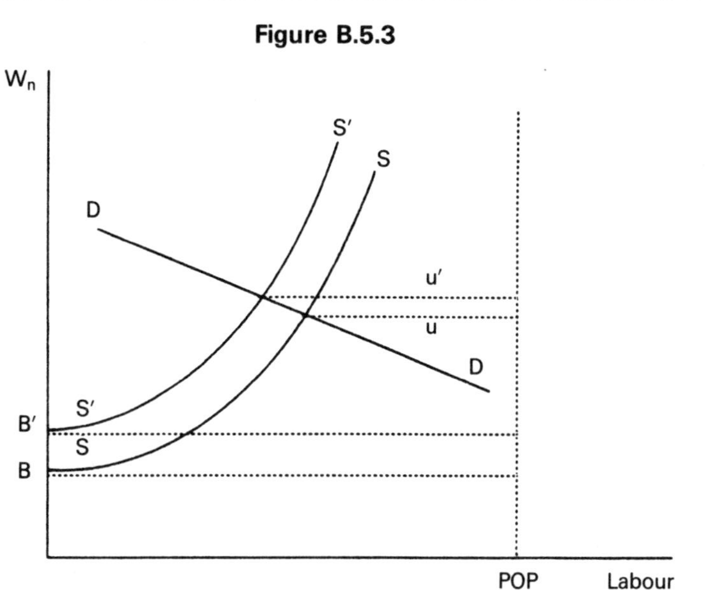

addition, world exports fell by 13 per cent between 1920 and 1922, which would lead to a leftward shift of DD (i.e., reducing the demand for labour).

union sector, which raises wages in both the union and non-union sectors. In the context of the inter-war period, workers who found themselves out of a job in the union sector had the choice of (i) searching for employment within that sector, (ii) taking work in the non-union sector, or (iii) going on some form of the dole—regular benefits, extended benefits, or some other form of outdoor relief once their claims had been exhausted. For many, the choice was going on the dole whilst waiting for an opening in the union sector.

An additional potential source of wage stickiness comes from the rôle of price expectations. Since unions converge on their target real wage by bargaining for money wages, this implies that an unexpected fall in the price level leads to an unexpected rise in the real wage. In a rational expectations view, this unanticipated element is strictly temporary. However, its effects may be long-lasting, depending on the speed of adjustment of the union nominal (and thus real) wage. This is an empirical issue which can be determined only by econometric investigation.

Finally, we come to the concept of equilibrium that underpins this model. There is no question that those workers who lost their jobs in the union sector would have preferred to work at the 'going wage' rate, rather than remain on the dole. Nevertheless, the going wage was in the union sector and a job in this sector was not a viable option; the union decision had rationed employment. This at least fits in with the findings of the Pilgrim Trust.[1] In his paper on long-term unemployment, Crafts writes:

> 'At the very least, investigations like those of the Pilgrim Trust and the Carnegie Trust make it clear that the vast majority of the unemployed regard their status as much inferior relative to the offer of a job at normal wages in their locality. . . .' (Crafts, 1987, p. 425.)

The term 'normal wages' is, of course, ambiguous, but since the concentration of the unemployed in the surveys was in the staple export trades, we can assume that these were, by and large, workers in the union sector. If the choice was between staying on the dole and working at normal (*union*) wages, then work was superior. If, on the other hand, the choice was between staying on the dole and working in the *non-union* sector, the choice for many, according to our evidence, was the dole.

(b) The USA

To apply our model to the USA, its structure must take into account the relevant institutional differences in that country. For example, government payments to the unemployed in the USA were neither automatic nor a matter of right. Relief payments, based on local need levels, were made to applicants from budgets which were fixed in the short run, and in most cases completely exhausted in the course of granting relief. This allows only two possibilities regarding the market for work relief. This market was either continuously in equilibrium or it was rationed (creating an excess supply of applicants). If the market for work relief cleared continuously, then all those who sought relief were able to obtain it. In this case, the supply of labour to the non-

[1] Pilgrim Trust (1938).

union private sector would have depended on the wage in the non-union private sector relative to the wage (relief payment) in the public relief sector, just as labour supply in the UK depended on private wages relative to unemployment benefits.

If the market for work relief were rationed, however, the supply of labour to the non-union private sector would have depended on the real wage relative to the *expected* benefit from the relief sector. Since the receipt of relief benefits was not a certainty, *expected* benefits would depend on *actual* benefits, weighted by the probability of securing a place in the relief sector. Models of search theory imply that in full equilibrium, the expected wage (adjusted for search costs) in the non-union private sector will equal the expected benefit from the relief sector.[1] That is, the wage adjusted for the costs of search will just equal the relief benefit adjusted for the costs of waiting. In principle, the unemployed worker had the option of looking for work in the non-union private sector or applying for work relief and waiting for an opening. In practice, he presumably would have done both. As in the UK, work in the union sector was not an option open to the unemployed worker who was effectively rationed by the unions.

Relief Budgets and Relief Recipients

One further aspect which needs to be modelled is the determination of the relief budget and, by implication, the number of places available for work relief. We assume that the relief budget for each state was determined by three factors. These are the level of benefit, which is given by local 'need levels',[2] the size of the population within the State, and local political pressure factors which influenced the distribution of federal monies. It follows that, on the one hand, a rise in benefits brought about by an increase in local needs levels will increase the budget. On the other hand, for a given budget, a rise in the benefit level means that fewer places are available for relief. This means that once the budget was determined, local relief agencies had the potential to

---

[1] See, for example, Stigler (1961).

[2] The Federal government required local relief authorities to establish 'need levels', which were supposed to reflect minimum standards of living for families of various sizes in the local area.

reduce the level of relief payments so as to absorb more applicants for relief.

Although local relief authorities established need levels, the federal government played a major rôle in determining the total size of each locality's relief budget. The combination of need levels and budget levels was not always consistent with the number of people who applied for relief each month. In particular, there is ample anecdotal evidence that many local authorities often did not have enough money to service all applicants. Rather than cut benefits per case, they sometimes turned applicants down. As a result, people applying for relief were not guaranteed its receipt, even if they were eminently qualified on paper.

In the light of the foregoing, the model is completed with the definition of *expected* benefits, which are *actual* benefits weighted by the probability of securing a place in the relief sector. If the total work-force is assumed to be made up of those employed in the private sector, those employed on relief projects and those who are unemployed, the probability of securing relief would be given by the proportion of workers not in private sector employment who are in receipt of relief.[1] If the market for relief had cleared continuously, then the probability of securing relief would have been 1; in fact it was considerably less than 1 during the 1930s.

A diagrammatic representation of the full model for the US case is outlined in Box 6 (below, p. 127). It is assumed that the market for relief was rationed and that the level of relief payments per person and relief places varied inversely. The diagram in Box 6 traces out the effect of an increase in the relief budget on private sector employment. It turns out that the overall effect on expected relief benefits and therefore on private sector employment will depend on the estimated parameters. A rise in the relief budget, holding the level of benefit per person constant, increases the number of places available for relief. Initially, this raises the probability of securing relief which increases expected benefits and the relative attractiveness of working in the relief sector rather than the non-union private

---

[1] Strictly speaking, it was possible for people with jobs to be in receipt of relief. This matter is discussed more fully below. For the moment, we simply assume that the number of such people was sufficiently small to be ignored.

BOX 6

Increase in the Relief Budget

Figure B.6:1 describes the effect of an increase in the budget for relief for a given level of relief payments. The increase in the budget is described by a shift in CD to C′D′. Initially, labour supply is described by SS, employment in the private sector is given by OE_0, the number on relief work is given by OC_0 and the number of unemployed is C_0U_0. Suppose the budget is expanded to absorb all the unemployed queuing for relief work so that $OC_1 = OU_0$. The increase in the number obtaining relief work increases the probability of obtaining relief, which raises expected benefits and shifts the supply schedule SS to S′S′. Employment in the private sector is consequently reduced to OE_1, the amount on relief work remains at OC_1, but unemployment is given by C_1U_1. The increase in expected benefits causes a substitution between the private sector and the queue for public relief.

Figure B.6.1

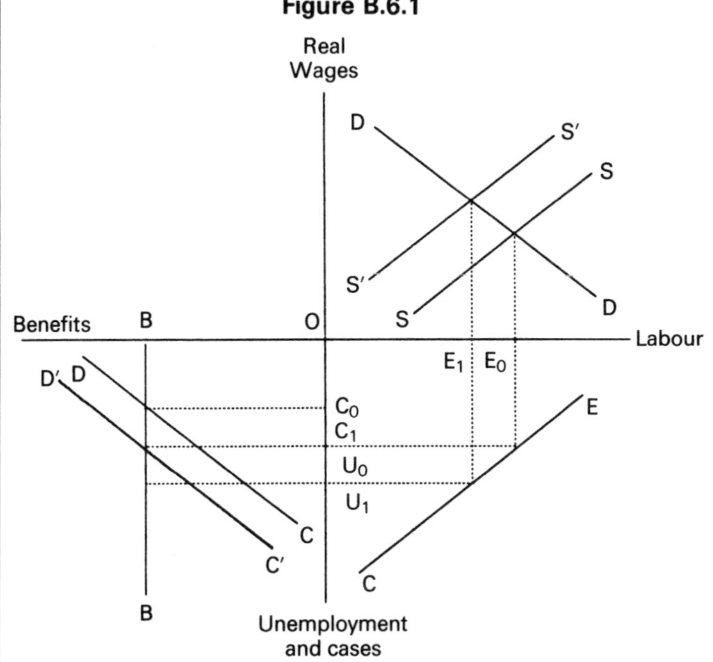

sector. The increase in the number of applicants for work relief will subsequently reduce the probability of securing relief. The net effect is to be determined empirically.

2. The Results

(a) The UK

The econometric results are presented in an Appendix to this Chapter (below, p. 144). We outline here the main features of our findings.

Despite the Keynesian folklore about the period, we found that a competitive market (neo-classical) model out-performed the Keynesian demand-constrained model, in terms of statistical fit. The theoretical specification of the demand for labour relates employment (or unemployment) to the real cost of labour, the real exchange rate, and the capital stock. Since data for the capital stock does not distinguish between the private and public sectors and, as always, the quality of capital stock figures is a major source of concern for all researchers using either contemporary or historical data,[1] a time trend was used to proxy the capital stock. The results confirm that employment was negatively related to real labour costs (real wages plus employers' contributions) and positively related to the real exchange rate.

The supply curve is estimated in terms of the real wage; that is, the supply of labour is expressed as a wage determination function—a specification that has been successfully applied to post-war UK data.[2] In summary, our findings show that the real level of unemployment benefits had a strong positive influence on real wages. We also found that there was a one-off decline in the union mark-up in the first three years of the 1920s. This explains the 10 per cent fall in real wages in 1921-23 at a time when the real value of benefits rose by over 50 per cent. Our findings also show that an unanticipated reduction in the price level caused a temporary increase in real wages.

(b) The USA

The model for the United States was estimated using *pooled* time-series and cross-section data. The data consisted of observations

---

[1] Feinstein (1972) estimates that the capital stock has a 10-25 per cent error.

[2] See Minford (1983).

for employment, output, wages, relief cases, and relief payments for the period 1932-39 for 48 states.[1] Pure time-series data consisted of the consumer price index, the average tax rate (government receipts as a proportion of national income), and union density. Pure cross-section data consisted of demographic variables affecting the supply of labour, and political bargaining factors affecting the budget determination function.

The results confirm that the demand for labour slopes downwards. Because cross-section data on the capital stock is not available, we could not test for the competitive market (neo-classical) model. However, as discussed earlier, it is clear that the US economy suffered stronger deflationary demand shocks than any other country during this period. Consequently we do not think that a demand-constrained Keynesian specification is inappropriate. The demand for labour is therefore specified as a derived demand—that is, it is contingent on the level of aggregate demand.

Like that of the UK, the US labour supply function was estimated as a real wage function. As a practical matter, the probability of obtaining unemployment benefits in the UK was unity.[2] This was not the case in the USA. Empirically, the measured probability of obtaining relief had a significant impact on the supply of labour, implying that the market for relief cases was not clearing.

The estimated results are presented in the Appendix to this Chapter. The main findings are that both the real level of relief and the probability of obtaining relief had a strong positive influence on the real wage. We also found that a significant 'mark-up' opened up between union and non-union wages in the USA during the 1930s. The economy-wide rate of unionisation in 1933 amounted to 11·3 per cent of the working population. It stayed roughly constant until 1937 when it rose to 22·6 per cent. The growing strength of unions during the thirties reflected both

---

[1] Data on recipients of relief were on a 'case' basis; each case was a family unit, and could consist of an individual, a family with only one member in the labour force, or a family with multiple labour force members.

[2] This conclusion should be tempered in accordance with the discussion in Benjamin and Kochin (1979a) regarding the operation of the Anomalies Regulations, and the discussion in Benjamin and Kochin (1982) regarding the impact of disallowances.

the National Industrial Recovery Act of 1933 and (more importantly in the long run) the National Labour Relations Act (Wagner Act) of 1935. The former Act recognised the right of employees to organise and bargain collectively, and the latter established a National Labour Relations Board for the purpose of ensuring that employers negotiated with union representatives. By 1939, the rate of unionisation was more than double its 1932 level, and union wages rose significantly relative to non-union wages.

We found no evidence of money wage rigidity. What this means is that, allowing for all other factors, a fall in the price level led to a commensurate fall in money wages. Thus, unlike in the UK, the US labour market was a lot more flexible and did not share the same degree of inertia in money wages. This could be due to the difference in the historical development and tradition of unions between the two countries. Although the legislation of the 1930s strengthened the position of the unions, union density in the USA was still considerably lower than that of the UK for much of the thirties.

Education and Migration

Several demographic factors influenced the supply of labour in the USA during this period. We found that the net migration of white workers into a state tended to raise average wages while the net migration of blacks tended to lower average wages. This can be explained by the skill differentials that must have existed between the two racial groups. On average, black workers were less skilled than white workers at this time and so had lower average wages. Another interpretation is that these variables reflect the impact of racial discrimination. Both explanations satisfy the folklore of the period and reinforce each other. Black workers were discriminated against because on average a black person signalled a lower level of productivity or skill in relation to an average white worker, although this would not be true for all workers of either race.

We also found that the higher the proportion of the population with high school education in a state, the lower the average wage in that state. We think that this variable is picking up other cross-sectional influences not modelled here. One possible interpretation is that states with a higher proportion of white-collar workers (positively correlated with education) had wages rising at a lower rate than the states with a higher proportion of blue-collar workers—that is to say, that blue-collar wages rose relatively to white-collar wages in this period. We think there are at least three plausible reasons for this phenomenon to have occurred in this period.

First, we know that the Wagner Act led to an increase in union organisation. Although we have allowed for the effects of the Wagner Act on the union mark-up by using union density as a proxy, we have not allowed for its effects on the distribution of wages. Union organisation was typically concentrated in the blue-collar sector, whereas white-collar workers were typically not unionised in this period. Union pressure was therefore able to raise the relative wage of blue-collar workers.

A *second* possible reason is that the wages of blue-collar workers are more cyclically sensitive. They would fall faster than wages of white-collar workers in a recession and rise faster in an upturn. The bottom of the recession in the USA was reached around the first half of 1933. The time-series sample we are using begins in 1933, and although there was a further recession in 1937-38, most of the period was one of prolonged upturn.

Third, since this was a period of widespread migration of rural workers, local wages became less subject to local monopsony pressure. Workers with low education were able to raise their relative wages because of the increased opportunity simply to migrate to neighbouring states.

Regarding the demand for relief workers by the relief sector, we find that the authorities did vary the level of relief to absorb more workers. Our estimates indicate that the quantity demanded for relief workers varied inversely with the average level of relief payments. We also find that several proxies for political pressure factors contributed to the determination of the state relief budget. States with a higher proportion of blacks—typically the Southern states—on average received less federal relief than states with a lower proportion of blacks; whether this reflected racial discrimination or not we do not know. An alternative explanation is that states with large numbers of blacks (i) tended to be lower-income states so had lower 'needs' levels, and (ii) these states were also agricultural, Southern states which were not hit as hard by the depression, and so were judged to be less in need. Similarly, the reason why the proportion of the farming population had a negative effect on the distribution of the budget could be due to differences in political pressure between farming states and states with large urban areas (which have more votes).

To sum up, the results confirm that demand curves slope downwards and lower real wages increase employment. They also show that, unlike the UK, aggregate demand was an important determinant of employment. This highlights the important differences in the conditions of the two economies. The contraction in aggregate demand played a much stronger part in explaining unemployment in the USA than in the UK. But, like the UK, the relief payments had an influence on the wage process and hindered what Clay (1929b) described as 'the natural plasticity' of wages to fall in a recession.

3. A Doleful Story

What effects did the level of benefits (relief) have on employment in the two countries? This question is answered by using the econometric model presented in the Appendix (below, p. 144) to evaluate the effects of the dole (relief) on real wages and employment.[1]

(a) The UK

Using some of the estimates from the UK model mentioned above, we can make significant progress in answering the question: How much did the dole raise the natural rate of unemployment? To do this we need to specify aggregate demand and supply relations that take into account the interaction between the real exchange rate and the demand for labour. These are taken from Matthews (1989b).

Basically, the real exchange rate (the inverse of competitiveness) is determined by unit labour costs, which in turn are given by the level of real wages. A rise in the real exchange rate (worsening of competitiveness) reduces exports and reduces aggregate demand; conversely, a rise in world trade increases export demand and raises aggregate demand. We can use this analysis to draw a link from the real level of benefits to real wages, through to

[1] We also use the results from a full macro-economic model of the UK inter-war period reported in Matthews (1989b) to evaluate the effect of the dole on the natural rate of unemployment.

Chart 4a:
Sterling/Dollar Real Exchange Rate, 1920-38
(1929 = 100, annual averages)

competitiveness and unemployment: a rise in real benefits worsens competitiveness and increases the natural rate of unemployment. A rise in world trade improves net trade and reduces the natural rate.

Charts 4a and 4b plot out two measures of the real exchange

Chart 4b:
Sterling Average Effective Real Exchange Rate, 1921-38
(1929 = 100, annual averages)

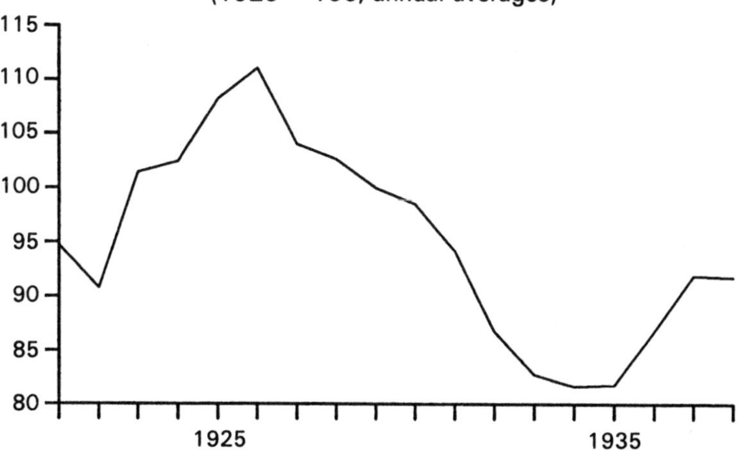

Chart 5:
Inter-war Employment in the UK, 1921-38
(millions)

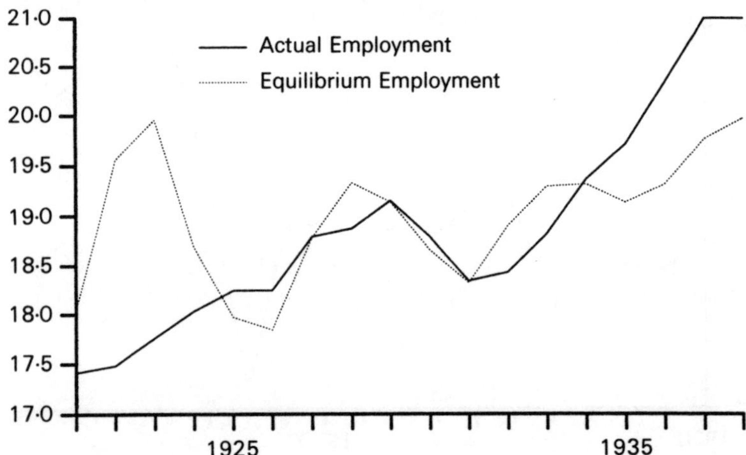

rate over the full period. The first chart is in terms of the dollar/sterling exchange rate and the second is in terms of a sterling effective exchange rate. The real exchange rate remained high during much of the twenties, fell in 1931 following the collapse of the Gold Standard, and then moved back up toward its pre-crash level in the remaining inter-war years. The appreciation was greater for the dollar/sterling real exchange rate than for the measure based on the effective exchange rate, but in both cases there was some rebound after 1932.[1]

World trade grew rapidly during the twenties. The growth in world exports from 1921 to 1929 averaged 11 per cent per year. World exports fell by 28 per cent over the next three years, however, and by 1938 had still not regained the level of 1929.[2] This meant that world demand contributed to UK growth in the 1920s and helped keep the natural rate of unemployment from rising. However, the natural rate rose following the collapse in world trade at the beginning of the 1930s.

The real level of unemployment benefits (using a fixed weight measure) rose by 57 per cent between 1921 and 1929. Real

[1] See Dimsdale (1981).

[2] Despite rising by 37 per cent between 1933 and 1938.

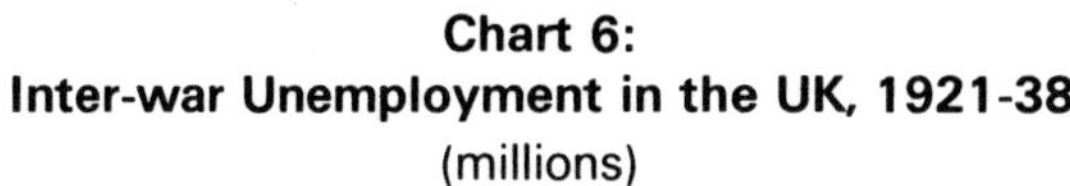

Chart 6:
Inter-war Unemployment in the UK, 1921-38
(millions)

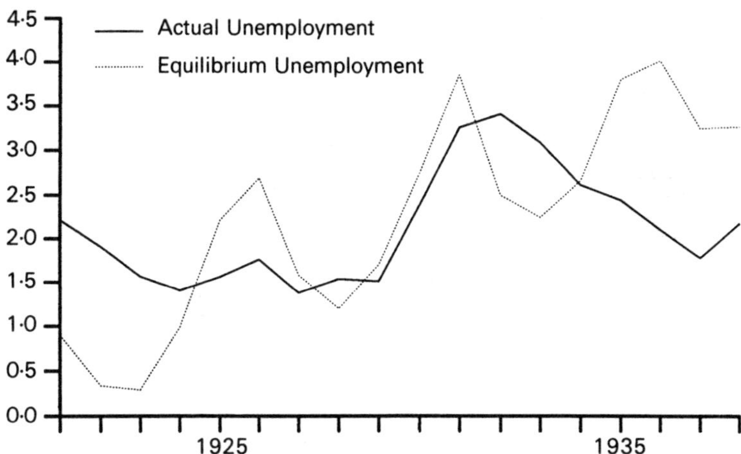

benefits rose by only 0·5 per cent between 1930 and 1932, following the MacDonald austerity measures, and between 1933 and 1938 they rose by only 3 per cent. This means that there was strong supply pressure during the 1920s which was only partially offset by a one-off reduction in the union mark-up, whereas the contribution of unemployment benefits to the natural rate of unemployment in the 1930s was moderate.

The Natural Rate of Unemployment

Armed with this analytical framework and the background on real benefits and real trade, we can now tackle the question: How much did the dole raise the natural (equilibrium) rate of unemployment? We plot the implied equilibrium level of employment and unemployment in Charts 5 and 6.

Focussing on unemployment (Chart 6), we see that actual unemployment was considerably higher than the natural (equilibrium) level during the first half of the 1920s. This conforms with the conventional view that monetary deflationary policies, undertaken to facilitate the 1925 return to gold, depressed the UK economy in the first half of the decade. By 1925, deflationary pressure had forced the price level down by 22 per cent relative to its 1921 level. Over the same period, the nominal unemployment

**Chart 7:
Contributions to the Natural Rate
of Unemployment in the UK, 1921-38**
(millions)

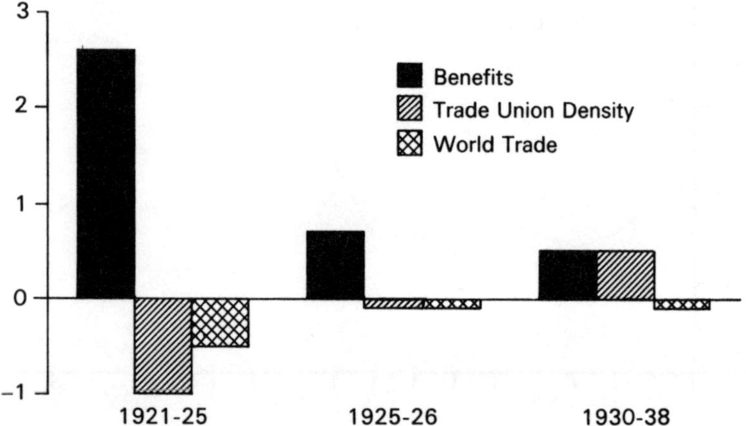

benefits level for a married man with two children rose by 60 per cent. The combination of these two forces raised the real value of benefits sharply. As a result, the natural level of unemployment rose to meet actual levels during the second half of the twenties.

The sharp contraction in world trade in 1931-32 produced a further increase in the natural level of unemployment during the early thirties. The latter years of the 1930s saw actual unemployment falling below the equilibrium level as demand expanded in response to the expansionary monetary policy of Hugh Dalton, the Chancellor of the Exchequer. The contributions of the various factors to the natural (equilibrium) level of unemployment are detailed in Chart 7.

The story that emerges from this exercise is that the dole had a major impact during the first half of the 1920s on the natural rate of unemployment—an impact that persisted through the rest of the inter-war years. Indeed, had not union density declined (a change that put downward pressure on real wages), the rise in the natural rate during the early twenties would have been even more severe. The real value of the dole continued to rise at a slower pace over the rest of the period, contributing to modest further increases in the natural rate. Nevertheless, after about

TABLE 9

THE EFFECTS OF A 10 PER CENT RISE IN THE REAL LEVEL OF RELIEF BENEFITS

Year	Cases (per State)	Employment (per State)
1	-3,030	-360
2	,,	-629
3	,,	-839
4	,,	-1,006
5	,,	-1,132
6	,,	-1,233
7	-3,030	-1,303

1926, subsequent changes in the natural rate were dominated by external (trade) and trend factors (capital accumulation).[1]

The analysis we have presented above leads us to the following conclusion: *If the real value of benefits had been maintained at the 1921 level, Britain would have entered the Second World War with an unemployment rate close to what existed immediately after the end of the First World War—which is to say, full employment by historical standards.*

(b) The USA

We now turn to the impact of the relief system on employment in the United States. We first consider a 10 per cent rise in real relief payments whilst holding the budget constant, and then we examine the effects of a 10 per cent rise in the relief budget whilst holding benefits constant.

Table 9 shows the effect of a 10 per cent rise in benefits on cases and employment,[2] *holding the total budget constant.* The figures in this Table are to be interpreted as follows. The impact of a 10 per cent rise in relief benefits holding the budget constant

[1] Which is to say that by 1926 the dole had established the 'million man army of the unemployed' which was to remain in place until called to serve in the Second World War.

[2] The effect on employment is calculated by applying the employment index to the 1930 Census estimates of employment.

was to add approximately 3,400 people to the unemployment queue of the average state (about 163,200 people nationwide) in the first year and about 4,300 per state (206,400 nationwide) by the seventh year. Initially, only a small proportion of these people (11 per cent = 360/3,390) were drawn to the unemployed from the ranks of the employed. The vast majority (89 per cent) were already unemployed but were expecting to obtain relief. The rise in the relief benefit, holding the budget constant, would have had the effect of reducing the number obtaining relief from the ranks of the unemployed by about 145,000 nationally. The long-run effects of higher relief benefits on private employment are far more significant. For example, by the end of the fourth year, roughly one-quarter of the increase in unemployment was drawn from private employment, and by the seventh year after a benefit increase, more than 30 per cent (1,300/4,330) of the addition to the unemployment queue consists of individuals who would have been gainfully employed in the private sector had benefits been 10 per cent lower.

The absolute size of the impact of a rise in relief benefits shown in Table 9 seems absurdly small at first glance. After all, the seventh year results—reduced employment of 13,000 persons per state—amounts to only a little over 600,000 fewer jobs for the economy as a whole. Pretty small beer, one might say—particularly since unemployment adjusting for relief workers averaged *7 million* over this period. However, this must be viewed in the light of the total rise in real relief payments during the period. On average, real relief payments per state soared by over 180 per cent between 1933 and 1939. Since our estimation period covers this entire span, the economic and historical significance of our results should thus be viewed in this light: *Roughly one-third of all persons attracted to the relief queue by higher benefits during the late thirties would have been employed in the private sector, but for those higher benefits.*

In Table 10 we present the effect of a 10 per cent increase in the availability of cases. An increase in the demand for cases increases the probability of securing relief, and thus increases expected benefits. The simulation shows that in the first year, while the relief rolls increased by nearly 8,800 per state, private employment fell by 2,260. However, by the seventh year, the increase in cases displaced nearly an equivalent number of

TABLE 10

THE EFFECTS OF A 10 PER CENT INCREASE IN THE AVAILABILITY OF CASES

Year	Cases (per State)	Employment (per State)
1	8,778	-2,256
2	,,	-3,992
3	,,	-5,325
4	,,	-6,356
5	,,	-7,153
6	,,	-7,765
7	8,778	-8,226

employees from private sector employment. The long effects of the relief programmes should thus be viewed in this manner: for every 10 'jobs' created by the relief programme, nine jobs were lost in the private sector.

We can use both these simulations to understand the overall effect of relief benefits on private sector employment. The annual percentage increase in the relief budget, in real terms, can be viewed as the percentage increase in cases plus the percentage increase in real relief per case. Thus we can isolate the effects on private sector employment of an increase in relief benefits (holding cases constant) from the effects of an increase in cases (holding real relief constant).[1]

In 1933, total unemployment including those on relief amounted to 12·8 million. The number in receipt of relief was 2·2 million. Our results suggest that the creation of 2·2 million jobs in the public relief sector crowded out nearly 730,000 jobs from the private sector. By 1939, total unemployment including those on relief had fallen to 9·5 million and the number in receipt of

[1] Data for the relief budget or its break-down into cases or relief per case in 1932 is not available. However, some data can be obtained on the total relief budget for 1931 (Bailey, 1983, Table 7, p. 51). The increase in the budget between 1931 and 1933 was 67 per cent. In the calculation of the crowding-out effects we assume that all of the increase in the budget went towards increasing the number on the relief roll rather than on increasing relief per case.

Chart 8:
Proportion of Private Sector Jobs Crowded Out by the Creation of Public Relief Jobs in the USA, 1933-39

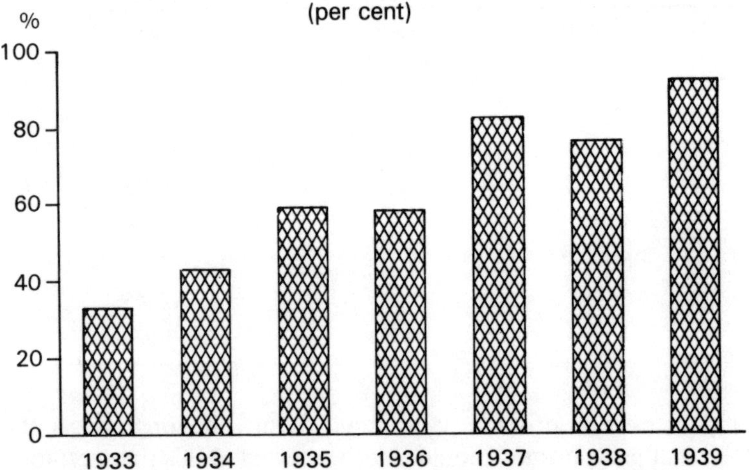

relief had increased to 3·3 million. Our results show that the creation of 3·3 million jobs in 1939 had crowded out 3 million jobs in the private sector. Chart 8 illustrates the proportion of private sector jobs lost for every job created in the public relief sector, over the years 1933-39. *The conclusion is that in 1933, for every three people taken off the unemployment queue an extra one joined it. By 1939, for every 10 people taken off the unemployment queue a further nine joined it!*

Transmission Mechanism: From Benefit (Relief) to Unemployment

It is important at this stage to understand the transmission mechanism from benefits or relief payments to unemployment. The analysis of the previous chapter and the statistical results in the Appendix give the impression of people coldly evaluating their marginal rate of substitution between income and leisure and comparing it with their alternative, and then opting to work or consume leisure (or in the case of the USA, to work or to apply for relief). *We should not be misled; the actual processes were far more subtle and complex.* For example, young men and women in the UK did not quit work as soon as they reached the age of 18 because benefits rose sharply at that age. Quitting would have cost them their benefits; so employers obliged large numbers of them by laying them off and replacing them with younger workers.

Consider, for example, the so-called 'voluntary' nature of the increases in unemployment rates observed to occur at ages 18 and 21. Relative to wages, unemployment benefits were lowest for juveniles (aged under 18), higher for people aged 18-20, and highest of all for people aged 21 or over.

When business is slack, employers are faced with a choice. Should they reduce hours of work or wages, or should they lay off workers? And if the second option is taken, which workers should be given the sack? The existence of unemployment benefits will alter the choices of employers in two ways: initially, they will be more likely to lay off their workers because the benefits make lay-offs less onerous for workers than they would be in the absence of benefits. We are not claiming that workers enjoy either wage cuts or lay-offs; the point is rather that, when faced with the prospect of one or the other, the existence of benefits payable for lay-offs (but not payable for wage cuts) means workers are better off if they are layed off rather than given wage cuts. To keep their workers happy, employers comply by laying off workers, thereby raising the unemployment rate.

Similarly, if benefits differ for different classes of workers, the structure of benefits will help determine the structure of lay-offs. In the absence of benefits, employers will adopt rules for determining the order in which workers will be layed off. If benefits are structured to favour particular sub-classes of workers, employers will have an incentive to alter their lay-off rules to take advantage of this structure. In the inter-war context, as already stated, benefits were low relative to wages for the youngest workers, higher for those aged 18-20, and highest of all for adults aged 21 and over. This structure of benefits encouraged employers to impose relatively more lay-offs on older workers and relatively fewer lay-offs on younger workers. As a result, the unemployment rate followed the same pattern as the generosity of benefits: it was lowest among juveniles, higher for people aged 18-20, and highest among adults. This positive association between unemployment benefits and unemployment rates almost certainly did not occur because large numbers of individuals quit their jobs at ages 18 or 21. After all, quitters were ineligible for benefits for six weeks. Instead, employers co-operated with workers by laying them off when the workers would be better off on the dole.

Certainly, from the perspective of the outside observer, and perhaps even when viewed by the individual worker, these lay-offs would be seen as being wholly 'involuntary'. Yet when viewed in the larger context of the implicit contract between employer and workers as a group, fine-tuning the lay-offs to fit the structure of benefits makes employer and employees better off than ignoring the structure of benefits. In this sense, the lay-offs and hence the ensuing unemployment are, at least in part, 'voluntary' (see also Feldstein, 1976).

Similarly, it would be a mistake to think that all persons on the dole preferred the dole to work. Although some surely did, as the Pilgrim Trust testified, there were many who would have gladly given up a life of leisure for work at the union wage-rate. But work in the union sector was not an option that was available. It was rationed by the unions. To say that some people would have preferred work at the union wage is simply another way of saying that some of the unemployed had a high 'reservation wage'. Evidence of this is rife in the Pilgrim Trust report:

> 'The man who was a boot and shoe operative, drawing the same rate of allowance as in the previous instance, said that he could have had a job some time since but that he refused to work below Trade Union rates ... he was not willing to work (in the phrase current in Liverpool) 'under the light'. A young Liverpool seaman ... said that he knew many who would take a job for 35/–, but he would take nothing under 45/– or 50/– for he believed he was worth that.' (Pilgrim Trust, 1938, p. 208.)

For those who faced poor earnings in work (in the non-union sector) compared to what they could get on the dole, the decision may not have been simply a question of dole *versus* work. Initially, people on the dole would have looked for work in their locality but found none in the union sector and little in the non-union sector that would have compensated them for their trouble, or they found few jobs that paid the same as their previous work income. After a time of searching they may have been sufficiently 'discouraged' to accept that their position was the best they could do and so became one of the long-term unemployed.

In the United States, we are not claiming that people quit private sector jobs to work for the WPA; instead, they refrained from re-entering private sector employment after being laid off, because of the WPA. The unemployed worker may not have coldly calculated the opportunity cost of working in the non-union sector against that of waiting in the relief queue, but the existence of the WPA 'safety net' made the prospect of pounding the pavement for a private sector job that paid little more a chilly prospect.

4. Conclusions

The availability of unemployment benefits in the UK and the existence of relief programmes in the USA contributed to the unemployment of the period. This much is no longer in doubt, at least as far as the UK is concerned. Virtually all researchers of the period accept that unemployment benefits had a rôle to play in the unemployment of the inter-war period. Differences do arise as to the exact magnitude of that impact. Benjamin and Kochin (1979a, 1982) reckon that, on average, the benefit system raised the rate of unemployment by around five to eight percentage points. *Our figures suggest that, if anything, this is a conservative estimate.* The exercise based on simulation analysis implies that the dole raised the equilibrium level of unemployment by an average of 1·8 million over the full period. If it had not been for offsetting positive forces from world trade, capital accumulation and the fall in union density, the 'Hungry Thirties' would have been even less appetising!

With the USA, it is clear that the effects of benefits on unemployment were much smaller. However, our results add greatly to our understanding of why real wages did not fall in the late thirties and why unemployment was so slow in coming down from its peak in 1933. By 1939, *per capita* output was only 4 per cent below its 1929 peak but the rate of unemployment was 17·2 per cent compared with 3·2 per cent in 1929. At least one conclusion is clear. The FERA and WPA programmes did prolong the manifestations of the Great Depression. In doing so they also transformed the attitudes of the American public to the rôle of government—from unobtrusive servant to active partner (or master)—the legacy of which is part and parcel of the current American political scene.

APPENDIX TO CHAPTER 5

Econometric Model

(a) The UK

The estimation of a demand for labour is based on the competitive market (neo-classical) model. We experimented with two dependent variables: the economy-wide level of employment given in Feinstein (1972), and the economy-wide level of unemployment. Our best estimates are presented in Table A.5:1.

The results for the employment function are broadly similar to previous findings, such as reported in Hatton (1988) and Beenstock and Warburton (1986a). The long-run wage elasticity

TABLE A.5:1

DEMAND FOR LABOUR: UK

Sample 1921-1938, Instrumental Variable Estimation: 't' values in parentheses

Dependent Variable: LEMP

13·296	−0·636LRWTB	+0·203RXR	+0·016TIME	−0·029D26
(16·03)	(4·29)	(3·73)	(8·00)	(1·88)

$R^2 = 0{\cdot}9438$, $d = 2{\cdot}2638$; $s = 0{\cdot}136$

Dependent Variable: LU

−43·090	+9·006LRWTB	−1·174RXR	−0·080TIME	+0·348D26
(5·07)	(5·94)	(2·11)	(3·85)	(2·21)

$R^2 = 0{\cdot}7877$, $d = 1{\cdot}9884$, $s = 1{\cdot}8$

d is the Durbin-Watson statistic and s is the standard error of the regression expressed as a percentage of the mean of the dependent variable

LEMP	= log of employment: source Feinstein (1972)
LU	= log of unemployment: source Feinstein
LRWTB	= LRW + TB
LRW	= log of real wages, average earnings and consumer price index: source Feinstein
TB	= average employer's contributions per employee as a percentage of the average wage: source Chapman (1953), p. 242
RXR	= log of real exchange rate defined as log (CPI) + log (EXCH) − log (CPIUS)
EXCH	= dollar/sterling exchange rate: source LCES
CPIUS	= US Consumer price index: source LCES
D26	= General Strike Dummy, 1926 = 1, 0 otherwise

TABLE A.5:2

SUPPLY OF LABOUR: UK

(*Real Wage Equation*)

Sample 1921-1938, Method of Estimation: Instrumental Variable; 't' values in parentheses

Dependent Variable: LRW

1·148	+0·146LBEN	+0·0088DTU(−1)	+0·711LRW(−1)	−0·441DLP
(2·25)	(3·19)	(3·65)	(6·65)	(3·05)

$R^2 = 0{\cdot}9298$, $d = 2{\cdot}3927$; $s = 0{\cdot}33$

LRW	= log of real wages, average earnings and consumer price index: source Feinstein
LBEN	= log of real benefits, calculated on a fixed weight basis. Benefits data: source Burns (1941), weights derived from Hatton (1980)
DTU	= Change in percentage union density constructed as union membership as a percentage of the employed labour force: source Pelling (1973)
DLP	= annual rate of inflation (CPI): source Feinstein

of demand for labour is −0·64 which compares with −0·57 obtained by Hatton (1988), while the real exchange rate elasticity of demand is 0·20 compared with Hatton's 0·38. The best estimates of the supply curve stated as a wage equation are presented in Table A.5:2. The estimated equation is well determined and satisfies the usual statistical criteria in as much as can be expected for such a short time-series data sample.

The wage data refer to average earnings from Feinstein (1972) and the benefit data were constructed on a fixed-weight basis from Hatton (1980). The real level of benefits was positive and significant but in keeping with other findings the level of employment (or unemployment) had no influence on real wages (see also Broadberry, 1986). That is to say, the supply of labour was perfectly elastic at the real wage. There are two reasons for this.

First, according to the standard type of trade union model employed in modelling the union sector, unemployment does not enter into the union's objective function: the union is simply a wage setter and the level of unemployment in the union sector is then given by the difference between the employer's demand for union labour and total union membership.

Second, in the non-union sector, the supply of labour becomes more elastic as the wage tends towards the benefit level. This is because benefits act as a floor to the wage rate. In the limit, when benefits equal wages, the amount of non-union labour supplied is zero. This implies that at high replacement rates, unemployment is unlikely to influence the wage. Replacement rates calculated on average earnings reached a peak of 57 per cent in 1936. Using earnings in manufacturing, the replacement rate reached a maximum of 69 per cent. Since these are based on combined (union plus non-union) earnings figures, there is a strong presumption that replacement rates for the non-union sector were even higher—indeed the Royal Commission on Unemployment Insurance found replacement rates in excess of 100 per cent for some non-union workers.

Theory tells us that the level of union density (the proportion of union members within the labour force) should be a significant determinant of real wages. We found that the rate of change of union density had a positive and significant effect. An examination of the union density data in Table 8 shows that the rate of unionisation fell sharply in the first three years of the 1920s, coinciding with an equally sharp fall in real wages. The rate of change of unionisation acts like a dummy variable which we can interpret as follows. The union mark-up fell in the first few years of the 1920s and then remained constant throughout the rest of the period. What this means is that the fall in the mark-up offset the sharp rise in real benefits in 1921-23 and pushed real wages down. After the initial fall in real wages, it was the rise in real benefits that explains the trend rise in real wages over the remainder of the period.

We also found some evidence of short-run money wage rigidity in that the inflation rate had a temporary but negative effect on real wages. This means that the tightening of monetary policy during this period, directly contributed—albeit temporarily—to the rise in real wages, and thus to unemployment.

How do our results compare with other recent findings? The estimated long-run elasticity of unemployment response to benefits, which can be calculated from Tables A.5:1 and A.5:2, turns out to be 4·55. This of course is only a partial statement because the real exchange rate which has a negative effect on unemployment (positive on employment) reacts positively to the real wage. Using estimates obtained by Matthews (1986a), the long-run elasticity of unemployment to unemployment benefits is calculated as 3·45. The most recent time-series estimates are from Dimsdale, Nickell and Horsewood (1989)—DMH for short. Using quarterly data for the period 1925(1) to 1938(4), DMH find a long-run response of unemployment to the replacement rate of 1·07—less than one-third of the result obtained in this study. There are two reasons for this difference.

Firstly, it is one of specification. DMH use the replacement rate in their wage equation whereas we use the real level of benefits. The argument for using the real level of benefits is that the replacement rate matters mostly to those on low wages and in unorganised trades, but the observed wage-rate refers to all workers. The wages of higher-paid workers and those in organised trades would be affected only insofar as an increase in the level of benefits filters through from the non-union sector via the union mark-up. Since the unions were weak in this period, we would expect workers at the bottom end of the income distribution to be considerably more influenced by benefits. The long-run response of average wages to benefits in Table A.5:2 is 0·51—a plausible estimate given the reasoning underlying the model.

The second major difference is with the sample size. DMH begin their estimation with 1925 rather than 1921, thereby precluding the period with the largest movement in real benefits and the replacement rate. This would bias their estimates downwards.

(b) The USA

Employment was measured by an index at the state level (constructed and reported in Wallis (1989)). Wage data were obtained by dividing total pay-roll by total employment (full- and part-time) per state from the Bureau of Labor Statistics (BLS) establishment sample. Aggregate demand is an index constructed from the industrial employment share weights, obtained from the 1930 and 1940 population censuses, and the BLS index of industrial employment. In essence, industrial employment shares at the state level (obtained from the Census) were used to weight national employment indices by industry—see Benjamin and Wallis (1980) for a discussion. Relief payments, case loads

TABLE A.5:3

DEMAND FOR LABOUR: USA

Instrumental Variable Estimation; sample (1933-1939) × 48 states; 't' values in parenthesis

Dependent Variable: LEMP

-200·0	-0·167LRW	+0·257LY	+0·799LEMP(-1)
(1·36)	(3·39)	(8·11)	(32·00)

$R^2 = 0{\cdot}8407$, $F = 583{\cdot}9$

LEMP	= log of employment (employment index, 1929 = 100) per state
LRW	= log of real wage relative to 1932 real wage
LY	= log of index of output (1929 = 100), per state

and relief budgets were obtained from the Final Statistical Report of the Federal Emergency Relief Administration. A complete relief payment series was obtained for the full estimation period, 1933-39, by splicing the FERA benefit series onto the WPA series. In essence, the 1936 figure for both programmes was weighted by the share of cases in each programme for that year. Both the wage and relief payments data were deflated by the consumer price index. The units of measurement for cases (family units) and employment (an index number) are different. Thus, the probability of obtaining relief was proxied by:

(Employment index)*(Total cases)/(Labour force)

Tables A.5:3-A.5:5 present the preferred results using instrumental variable estimation in the case of both the demand for and the supply of labour.

Employment is positively related to output and negatively related to the real wage. A lag in the level of employment is included to account for long-run adjustment.

As in the UK, employment did not contribute to the explanation of real wages. It is likely that employment would be a significant determinant but for co-linearity with the probability term which by construction includes employment. Restricting the coefficient on π to equal that on benefits produced more encouraging results but for purposes of simulation we remain with the unrestricted estimates. Unlike the results for the UK, the *level* of union density was a significant determinant.

TABLE A.5:4

SUPPLY OF LABOUR: USA

Instrumental Variable Estimation; sample (1933-1939) × 48 states; 't' values in parentheses

Dependent Variable: LRW

0·994	+0·062LEMP	+0·080LB	+0·159π	+0·003UNR
(1·94)	(0·062)	(4·56)	(3·92)	(2·42)

-0·358LEDUC	+453·05MW	-3592·97MB
(3·18)	(2·86)	(3·28)

$R^2 = 0{\cdot}2942$, $F = 19{\cdot}5$

LB	= log of relief benefits per relief case deflated by the economy wide consumer price index
π	= measure of probability of securing relief, measured as log of Cases divided by 1930 Census of work force multiplied by employment
UNR	= Union density (economy-wide)
LEDUC	= Years of completed schooling per state (cross-section)
MW	= net migration of white population per state
MB	= net migration of blacks per state

The model for the determination of the demand for relief workers by the public relief sector begins with the determination of the relief budget. We assume that the relief budget (X) is determined by the 'needs' levels as reflected in the level of relief per case (B), the size of the population of the state (P), and political and demographic factors (Z). Thus:

$$X = X(B, P, Z) \quad \text{where } \delta X/\delta B > 0,\ \delta X/\delta P > 0$$

By definition $C = X/B$ therefore $C = X(B,P,Z)/B$ and $\delta C/\delta B < 0$, provided that $\{(\delta X/\delta B) - C\}/B < 0$.

A representative result for the demand for case workers is presented in Table A.5:5. Real benefits appear negative and significant but clearly the most significant explanatory variable is population size.

Other variables that contributed to the explanation were federal tax receipts as a proportion of lagged National Income (Tax), which acts as a proxy for the federal budget constraint, the proportion of blacks in a state (PB), the proportion of the farming

TABLE A.5:5

DEMAND FOR RELIEF WORKERS: USA

Ordinary Least Squares Estimation; sample (1933-1939) × 48 states; 't' values in parentheses

Dependent Variable: LCASE

-2·4070	-0·3454LB	+7·0314TAX	-0·7043PB	-1·5117F30
(5·23)	(6·29)	(3·65)	(7·84)	(7·30)
-3·0278DINC	+1·0303LPOP			
(7·08)	(54·42)			

$R^2 = 0{\cdot}9183$, $F = 616{\cdot}00$

LCASE	= log of number of cases per state
TAX	= Federal tax revenue as a percentage of previous year national income
PB	= Proportion of black population per state
F30	= Proportion of farming population per state
DINC	= Change in per capita income per state
LPOP	= log of population per state

population (F30), and a measure of local needs levels proxied by the change in *per capita* income (DINC).

The estimated elasticity of demand for relief workers at -0·345 shows that the demand for relief workers was inelastic. What this means is that a unit rise in benefit relief reduces relief cases by proportionately less and therefore raises expected benefits.

6

THE LESSONS OF HISTORY

Revolutions and Revaluations

WE STUDY HISTORY for its lessons. In this dimension, the inter-war years were rich. They were years of tumult; as such, they offered both prospect and problem to contemporary observers and to analysts who followed. Statisticians and scientists alike greet 'outliers'—unusual events—with both hope and fear, for such events are, by definition, rife with information. They offer the opportunity to subject accepted modes of thought to stringent new tests; if the tests are met successfully there is renewed confidence that these modes are useful ways of thinking. But if the existing theories are flawed, then their weaknesses are most likely to be exposed. If this is the outcome, then the revelation is likely to produce both the stimulus and the opportunity to develop new theories. The stage is set, as it were, for a scientific revolution. Yet revolutions in science can be every bit as dangerous as those in the political sphere—displacing more than was bargained for, and creating more than was intended.

The century that preceded the First World War was one of unsurpassed prosperity and progress on both sides of the Atlantic. Intellectually, the great economists of that century had produced a bountiful crop from the seeds planted by Adam Smith. Politically, the English-speaking governments on both sides of the Atlantic had matured into confident instruments of wisdom, compassion and progressive thinking. The tumult of the twenties and thirties shattered that confidence; it forced economists to reexamine the fruits of their labours, and, ultimately, induced intellectuals and politicians alike radically to modify their views of the world. The *gestalt* that emerged from the thirties—that government could and must manage the economy—reigned until it too was challenged—by the tumult of the seventies. Our work on the inter-war years can thus be regarded as complementary to the rethinking of the post-war years that has taken place over the last decade. The message from both bodies of research is that the lessons learnt 60 years ago may have been less valid and far less valuable than they were originally seen to be.

Accompanying this message is a second lesson, one that is maddeningly difficult to get politicians to remember in the heat of battle. Keynes's justly famous allegory of the Castor Oil/Bismuth cycle was fundamentally meant to urge patience on the part of policy-makers. Our point is rather different, yet parallel; Keynes presumed politicians who understood the direction of influence of their actions, but who refused to wait until administering more of the same. Much of our story of the inter-war years, however, is about policy-makers who did not fully understand the consequences of their actions, and so not only administered more of the same, but also more of just about everything—so as to do *something, anything.* Too much of a bad thing must surely be bad, but there is some presumption that too much of a good thing is even worse—if for no other reason than that the initial pleasure associated with a good thing is lost. As we shall subsequently see, the importance of understanding the consequences of one's actions may be the most urgent lesson of our story for contemporary policy-makers.

Economists' Tools and 'Facts'

Our final message is perhaps a bit more arcane and inward-looking. Over the past 60 years there has been an explosive growth in the application of statistical and mathematical tools in economics. This growth has engendered rapid advances in our understanding of the world. Yet it has also changed the way economists view facts, theories, and their interrelationships. Advances in econometrics have drastically reduced the costs of producing new 'facts' (read: statistical relationships); similar advances in mathematical economics have likewise reduced the costs of producing new theories (read: mathematical models). As a consequence, the currencies of our realm have become devalued.

In the time of Smith, or of Marshall, facts did not qualify as such until they had become matters of common observation—scrutinised often and carefully enough to be widely accepted as verified. Theories were developed only in consultation with well-established facts, and were carefully examined for harmony both with existing facts and with accepted theories. New facts were intensely assayed *vis-à-vis* their own veracity, as well as for their consonance with the existing paradigm—a paradigm that viewed fact and theory as integrated strands of a single fabric.

Perhaps importantly because the inter-war years were so traumatic, this process faltered in the face of events in the twenties and thirties. Despite efforts to fit the facts into the existing paradigm, the magnitude and duration of unemployment during these years quite naturally led to efforts to modify existing modes of thought. Yet the very analytical tools that enabled Hicks and Samuelson so eloquently to express and extend the classical paradigm also enabled them and their followers rapidly to distil an immensely tractable version of the embryonic, competing theory offered by Keynes. Similarly, the development of the econometric tools that produced Fisher's findings of an apparent inverse relationship between wages and unemployment (familiarly known on this side of the Atlantic as the Phillips Curve), also enabled a quick patchwork of apparent facts in support of the new theories that were developed.

In effect, the technological innovations seemingly made possible easy answers to difficult questions; and in the process, the time-honoured methods of scrutinising the *fabric* of fact and theory were laid aside. Along the way, important elements of the body of knowledge built upon those methods were discarded. The contemporary predilection, at least among UK economists, for the application of econometric testing has led to the development of an agnostic approach, wherein the data are allowed to speak for themselves. In this sense, the technology of the science altered the course of the science: economists appear to have lost the art of binding together the fabric of their facts and theories into a coherent story—a loss which has diminished the usefulness of the discipline, both as a scientific endeavour and as a tool for policy-makers.[1]

The Present as History

Of the three lessons woven through our work in this book, it is the second—the importance of understanding the consequences of policy—that we wish to emphasise.[2] Fortunately, recent British governments have been kind enough to provide us with a contemporary experiment which confirms our arguments that

(i) policies are often (routinely?) implemented without a full appreciation of their likely consequences, and

(ii) results are unnecessary costs, confusion, and the application of 'corrective' policies that may have little to do with the root of the original problem.

Equivalently, the iatrogenic (an ailment caused by the treatment) maladies first identified by Keynes in his tale of the Castor Oil/ Bismuth cycle are far more pervasive than even he imagined.

The specific issue that stimulates our interest is the level of unemployment among juveniles. During the inter-war years, juvenile unemployment was the sole, feeble light in the Stygian darkness enveloping the British labour market. Although subject to the vagaries of the business cycle, the rate of juvenile unemployment was markedly lower than the aggregate unemployment rate—about two-thirds lower. Indeed, juvenile unemployment during the inter-war period looked remarkably like the total unemployment rate had looked before the First World War.

As Benjamin and Kochin (1979a, 1979b) have argued, and we have reiterated earlier in this volume, there appears to be a remarkably simple explanation for this pattern of juvenile unemployment: during the inter-war years, juveniles were fundamentally insulated from the effects of the unemployment insurance system, both by the low level of benefits payable to them, and by the contributory requirements that made it difficult for new

[1] A relatively recent development that has gone a long way in re-establishing the discipline as a useful tool for analysis and policy has the been the emergence of the New Classical/Supply-side school of thought.

[2] The other two lessons are no less important, but they are better addressed in the scientific journals.

entrants to the labour market to attain eligibility for any benefits during their first two years in the system.[1]

The initial post-war experience in Britain offered striking confirmation of this explanation: for the first 20 years after the Second World War, unemployment benefits were sufficiently low as to make the system an unattractive alternative to work for workers of *all* ages. During the same period, unemployment rates for both juveniles and adults were far below inter-war rates; more importantly, during this period in which the insurance system seems to have had no effect on the choice between employment and unemployment, the unemployment rates for adults and juveniles were virtually identical. This, of course, is what would be expected if the inter-war disparity between adult and juvenile unemployment was due to the differential impact of the insurance system on the two groups.[2]

In 1966, the British unemployment insurance system underwent a fundamental transformation. A system that had been conceived, viewed, and operated as an *insurance* system was transformed into a *guaranteed income* system. In short, the passage of the National Insurance and Supplementary Benefits Act of 1966 brought a change in British social policy of a magnitude that rivalled the passage of the Unemployment Insurance Act of 1920. Flat-rate unemployment benefits were raised sharply relative to wages and an additional earnings-related supplement was introduced. 'National Assistance' became 'Supplementary Benefits' and benefits under this scheme were increased relative even to the high and rising level of unemployment benefits.

The decade that followed witnessed a progressive liberalisation of the system. Existing benefits were raised in real terms, new benefits were introduced, and claims procedures were simplified. This liberalisation was accompanied by national advertising campaigns that extolled supplementary benefits as 'Social

---

[1] Eichengreen (1987b) suggests that the lower cyclical sensitivity of juvenile unemployment in the thirties is to do with the application of 'inverse-seniority lay-off rules'—meaning that senior (more experienced) workers would be laid off before junior (inexperienced) workers. Such an explanation not only strains credibility but also runs counter to the usual 'first-in-last-out' rule implicit in labour organisation theory. (See Reder, 1958, p. 189, or Addison and Siebert, 1979, pp. 304-08.)

[2] See Benjamin and Kochin (1982) for a complete discussion.

Security's Best Buy', and the publication of pamphlets that explained the plethora of benefits available and encouraged people to apply. This process of liberalisation accelerated in about 1973, and by the late seventies the combination of the unemployment insurance and supplementary benefits systems was beginning to look much like the unemployment insurance system of the late 1930s. So too was the unemployment rate, which hit levels not witnessed since before the Second World War.

The Tripling of Juvenile Unemployment

The rôle of the post-1966 rise in benefits and system liberalisation in raising the unemployment rate in Britain has been amply documented by Minford *et al.* (1985), and by others.[1] What has largely escaped attention, however, has been the sea-change in *juvenile* unemployment that took place during the seventies. Over the eight years from 1966 to 1973, the juvenile unemployment rate was slightly higher than the total unemployment rate (3·1 per cent *vs.* 2·4 per cent), an unremarkable difference considering the large numbers of 'baby-boom' youngsters successfully absorbed by the labour market. Over the *next* eight years (1974 to 1981) the juvenile unemployment rate soared to *three times* the total rate (17·3 per cent *vs.* 5·8 per cent). A group whose unemployment experience between the wars was one of the few welcome sights, and whose unemployment in the post-war years had been comparable to that of the rest of the population, suddenly became the eyesore of the labour market, seemingly unable to get or hold jobs. What happened?[2]

To begin to appreciate the answer, we must go back in time. Since the inter-war years and before, the process of entry into the labour force by young people has been remarkably stable. Upon

[1] The rôle of unemployment benefits is now an accepted part of mainstream European and UK economic thinking. The debate has shifted towards the empirical questions of parameter size and long-run effects. The most recent work in this area is Jackman, Layard, Nickell and Wadwhani (1989).

[2] A fairly recent study by the Department of Employment (Wells, 1983) argues that the period 1969-81 was one of relative scarcity of juvenile labour causing an increase in their relative earnings. Although the study recognises that replacement rates for juveniles increased in this period (p. 28), it skirts around the issue of benefits and fails to pin-point it as a major factor.

reaching the Spring of the year in which they have attained school-leaving age (SLA), youngsters not planning on further education have taken their examinations and proceeded to enjoy one last summer vacation. Then in September, after examination results have been announced, they set about obtaining employment. Although 'unemployed', in the sense that they had completed their schooling and did not yet have jobs, most of these youngsters did not show up on the official figures during that first summer: employers were not inclined to hire until examination results were known in late summer, and youngsters were not inclined to register at the Labour Exchanges until there was some prospect of employment. Moreover, these youngsters had no employment experience that might qualify them for unemployment benefits, and even after supplementary benefits were introduced they were too young (at age 15) to qualify. Hence, there were no benefit programmes that might induce them to register at the labour exchanges during the first summer out of school.

Matters began to change in the September of 1972 with the raising of the school-leaving age to 16. The initial impact was exactly what one might have expected: the 15-year-olds who would have entered the labour market as the 'Class of 73' did not do so, required as they were to complete an additional year of schooling. Thus, juvenile employment and unemployment in 1973 fell sharply. The following year (1974) this delayed class entered the labour market, and juvenile employment and unemployment rose. But the 'Class of 74' learned an important lesson, one apparently overlooked by the decision-makers who had raised the SLA: by entering the labour force when they were 16 rather than 15, they were immediately eligible for *supplementary benefits* during their last summer vacation.

This was a lesson that was not lost on the 'Class of 75'. Upon completing their GCE/CSE examinations, school-leavers immediately began registering at the labour exchanges in record numbers in the summer of 1975. The reason was not a sudden change in the hiring practices of employers, nor foolish optimism on the part of the new labour market entrants. It was instead the fact that registration was required for them to collect the supplementary benefits that would finance that last summer vacation. 'Unemployment' among juveniles soared, not because of a sudden lack of job alternatives, but because school-leavers were being *paid* to show up on the rolls of the unemployed—despite the fact that they and everyone else knew that few, if any, jobs would be forthcoming until September.

The members of the Class of 1975 were no more (and no less) 'unemployed' than were the members of, say, the Class of 1970 or the Class of 1960. The difference was this: since they were 16 at the time of school-leaving, they were eligible for supplementary benefits if they registered as unemployed. And register they did; over the years from 1967 to 1974, the mid-year (July) count of unemployed school-leavers had averaged 11,325; in 1975 the count soared to 55,300—triple the *highest* number that had ever been counted. By the next summer, the figures were staggering: the 1976 mid-year count revealed 199,400 unemployed school-leavers! And, of course, many of the young people who had so enjoyed their vacation found that they *liked* paid vacations. Thus, when September rolled around they were suddenly much less inclined to take up jobs—at least at the wage-rates previously offered them. And since employers had no reason to think that they were any more productive than before, they were not inclined to offer wage-rates sufficient to dislodge the youngsters from the rolls. September hirings fell sharply, and juvenile unemployment had suddenly become a problem.

Government's Response and Its Effects

The government responded swiftly and, seemingly, sensibly. The regulations for the receipt of supplementary benefits were changed to require school-leavers to sit out a term before receiving supplementary benefits. Presumably, two consequences were intended. Since the school-leavers would not spend the summer after school acclimatising themselves to living on supplementary benefits, they would be more likely to accept jobs in September. Moreover, fewer of them would be induced to sign the registers solely to collect supplementary benefits, so that the mid-year count of the unemployed would be reduced.

Although both of these effects no doubt occurred, thousands of school-leavers took a different course. They determined that if they dropped out of school prior to Easter, under the terms of the new regulations they would be eligible for supplementary benefits at the *beginning* (rather than the end) of the summer.

Enough school-leavers took this route so that, although the regulations *slowed* the rise in juvenile unemployment, the rise continued. Perhaps more importantly, for thousands of school-leavers the long-term results were to prove far more costly. By dropping out before Easter, they failed to take their GCE/CSE examinations, which in turn made them far less valuable to employers when the September hiring season started. Thus began a vicious circle, for when they failed to gain employment in September of their school-leaving year, their skills began to deteriorate relative to the skills of their peers, making their attainable wages even less attractive relative to supplementary benefits.

The icing on the cake—as if any were needed—stemmed from the reduction in the age of majority (from 21 to 18) which had taken place in 1969. Since people aged 18-20 were thenceforth considered 'adults', it seemed only reasonable that collective bargaining agreements and minimum wage arrangements be modified to elevate the wages of workers in this age-bracket to adult status. Between 1970 and 1975 the proportion of employed persons aged 18-20 subject to adult pay scales rose from approximately 18 per cent to more than 55 per cent; and by 1980 more than *two-thirds* of workers aged 18-20 were receiving adult pay. For those individuals who found jobs at adult scales, the results were rewarding: altogether during the first half of the 1970s, the average wages of workers aged 18-20 rose roughly 20 per cent relative to the wages of workers aged 21 and over.

But the application of adult pay scales to people aged 18-20 had its costs. The mere fact that the legal age of majority had changed did not make 18-20-year-olds any more productive. Thus, the spread of adult wage scales to this age-bracket simply raised the cost to employers of hiring these workers, compared to the cost of hiring workers over the age of 21. The net effect was a decline in employment for people aged 18-20, and a rise in their unemployment rates.

By the latter half of the decade, the employment situation worsened even more for people in this age category, as the school-leaving classes of 1975 and beyond—many of whose members had by-passed their public examinations—reached the age of 18. They found diminished skills even less valuable relative to adult pay scales, fashioned with the skills of better-educated, more experienced workers in mind. As the decade of the seventies came to a close, the sharp rise in unemployment that spread among 16- and 17-year-olds two or three years before swept through the ranks of those aged 18 to 20. By 1981, unemployment among all people under the age of 21 hovered around 25 per cent. A substantial portion of an entire generation was faced with the prospect of a lifetime with skills that merited wages little better than supplementary benefits—and thus little incentive to do more than collect those benefits.[1]

History as Future

In research detailed elsewhere,[2] we estimate that, while cyclical factors and other trend factors in common with aggregate unemployment accounted for much of the rise in juvenile unemployment during the seventies, roughly *one-half* of the rise was produced by the increase in the school-leaving age, acting in conjunction with increases in supplementary and unemployment benefits payable to this group. Moreover, although we have not attempted to track the long impact on the labour force prospects of these individuals, there can be little doubt that it has been severe.

The early years of labour force attachment are pivotal to long-run labour force success; these are years in which individuals are at peak levels of learning capacity, and years in which the most fundamental aspects of successful job performance are taught. The ages from 16 to 21 are the time in which the new entrants to the labour force are transformed from juvenile students into adult workers. For thousands of the members of the 'Class of 75', and tens of thousands of the members of the classes that followed them during the seventies and early eighties, this transformation never took place. These young people, individuals who are now in their late twenties and early thirties, were instead learning how to 'work the system': how to squeeze the most out

[1] Many (but not necessarily all) of those who chose not to take examinations because of the attractiveness of the dole probably would have scored poorly had they taken the exams. This fact simply means that the damage done by the policy is less than what it would have been if, say, all potential Oxbridge candidates were prohibited from taking their GCE/CSEs.

[2] Benjamin and Matthews (1990), 'Juvenile Unemployment and the School Leaving Age' (mimeo).

of Britain's welfare system. And while they were doing so, their socially productive job skills were continuing to decay. It is by now unlikely that many of these individuals will ever become fully integrated members of the labour force.

In this dimension, the social and economic damage wrought by the National Insurance and Supplementary Benefits Act of 1966 promises to exceed by far the damage wrought by the Unemployment Insurance Act of 1920. During the inter-war years, juveniles were insulated from the effects of the insurance, and those aged 18-20 largely so, until they became eligible for adult benefits. The work experience which they enjoyed from age 14 (the school-leaving age through most of the period) to age 21 (when adult benefits became operative) served as a foundation for them throughout their careers.

Just as importantly, the 'mind-set' of participants in the inter-war system was, through much of the period, entirely different from the mind-set of today's recipients of unemployment and supplementary benefits. The inter-war system was generally perceived as being what it had been established to be: an *insurance* system, the benefits of which accrued to those who had earned them as a result of working. To be sure, by the end of the inter-war period 'need' had replaced insurance as the criterion and benefits could, in fact, be collected indefinitely. And it was also true that the system was heavily subsidised from the general revenues of the Exchequer, making it far less of an insurance system than originally intended. Nevertheless, even those who 'abused' the system perceived their 'right' to do so as deriving from the fact that they were, after all, *workers*. By far the most prevalent form of unemployment consisted of intermittent spells involving alternating days or weeks of work interspersed by short periods on the dole. The '15 per cent unemployment' of the period was much closer to a hypothetical world in which all of the workers were unemployed 15 per cent of the time than it was to a world in which 15 per cent of the workers were unemployed all of the time. As a result, workers not only learned the fundamental job skills they required while they were young; they kept those skills as they passed through their careers.

The system confronting the 'children of the seventies' and, to a lesser extent, those of the eighties, has been fundamentally different. 'Insurance' still appears in the title of the legislation, but it has been supplemented (and in the minds of many, supplanted) by 'Benefits'. The mind-set of today once again follows that of the system which engendered it: benefits are a matter of *right*, earned not by virtue of work, but due in the course of mere existence, because one has reached a magic age, or simply cleared some administrative hurdle. That this right begins at age 16 means that no early work experience is acquired to enjoy it. And since it continues thereafter largely independent of one's work-force attachment, there is little incentive to re-establish that attachment once it is broken. Even the word '*Un*employment' has been removed from the title of the legislation, as if to suggest that *em*ployment has at last become irrelevant. For tens of thousands of Britons, 'XX per cent unemployment' has come to mean that XX per cent of the work-force is continually unemployed and rapidly becoming unemployable.

The Present as Future

The severity of juvenile unemployment became readily apparent by the early 1980s and the government moved to address it by instituting the Youth Training Scheme (YTS) in 1982 to replace the ineffective Youth Opportunity Programme (YOP). The scheme was intended to provide job training for school-leavers and in 1986, it was extended to provide a two-year structured period of training and job experience. Recent legislation (1988) went further by making YTS the only feasible way young people can be in receipt of income support. Under this scheme, juveniles must agree to participate in a training and job placement programme as a condition of benefit-receipt. At least in part, one must view this programme as a reaction to an underlying diagnosis:

(i) juveniles are unemployed because they have no marketable skills;

(ii) they cannot afford to get these skills on their own, and employers will not provide the training out of the goodness of their hearts;

(iii) therefore, the government must step in to provide the requisite training.

Thus, *more government training means less unemployment.*

The element of compulsion in the YTS (now known as Youth Training) as a means of receiving any form of benefits, may have the effect of inducing some youngsters to move into gainful employment directly. We can only wait for the results of future Labour Force Surveys. But, whatever the motivation or long-term prognosis for this programme, some movement of this sort is the almost inevitable short-term outcome of a scheme such as this: simply the requirement that youngsters endure the training will convince some of them that the dole is no longer worth the effort. What concerns us is that the programme may be fundamentally misdirected, and that its long-run benefits may prove to be scant indeed.

In our view, the 'lack of skills' on the part of juveniles is better viewed as a *symptom* of the problem, rather than its source. Although we rarely think explicitly of children and young adults as calculating, rational decision-makers, there is little doubt that they are aware of the costs and benefits of their actions—that is, of the incentives they face. (Indeed, why else would we bother to punish them when they are bad, and reward them when they are good?) Beginning with the decisions they make about how hard they study in school, and whether or not they take their GCSEs, continuing through their initial efforts to find employment, and extending even to their efforts in government training schemes, the incentives for tens of thousands of young people all point in one direction—dole, not work. Until and unless the benefits of Britain's welfare system in the 1990s are less than the prospective pay cheques (*net* of taxes and the disutility of work) of young people, the 'training' they receive in government schemes will have no more impact on their long-run employment choices than did the 10 or 12 years they spent in the school system.

US Experience with CETA: $55 Billion Wasted?

This simple lesson is one that it took the United States eight years and $55 billion to learn with the Comprehensive Employment and Training Act (CETA). This programme, in operation from 1973 until 1981, was targeted at individuals who typically were quite similar to those targeted by the YOP, YTS, YT programmes: young, unskilled, secondary school drop-outs, many of whom were eligible for some form of government welfare payments. Almost *uniformly*, the results of the various 'training' schemes tried under CETA *failed* to raise either the long-run employment rates or wage-rates of the target groups. In effect, virtually the entire $55 billion were wasted.

In response to CETA's failure, the programme was replaced by the Job Training Partnership Act (JTPA). The long-run effects of this programme, which did not become fully operational until 1984, are not yet known. There is some evidence that it is an improvement over CETA, and it appears clear that the successes to date have arisen from the fundamentally different structure of the programme. Under JTPA the government is out of the 'training' business; instead the programme's funds are dispersed to programmes that are designed and largely run by the private sector.

Conclusion

The simple fact is that individuals do what they *choose* to do, and they make those choices in the light of self-interest as perceived by them. We may not like those choices, but it will do little good to treat the symptoms of their choices instead of the causes. Prospective workers eschew opportunities to become skilled because it is not worth their while, and firms choose not to subsidise training because it is not worth their while. Ultimately, then, young people choose unemployment because it is the rational, self-interested choice for them to make. In this regard, we can state it no better than Edwin Cannan did more than 60 years ago:

> 'The endowment of unemployment isn't made any better by calling it insurance: fire insurance wouldn't do if you let people set their property on fire and keep it burning on condition of signing their names once a week at the insurance office.' (Cannan (1928), p. 398.)

We are not, nor was Cannan, advocating the abolition of social insurance. The point instead is that it, like all government policies, has costs as well as benefits. Until and unless policy-makers realise the full implications of what they do, those costs will be higher than they need or ought to be, and iatrogenic economic maladies will be the rule rather than the exception. And in the meantime, economists will make a living putting out fires.

REFERENCES AND SELECT BIBLIOGRAPHY

Addison, J. T., and W. S. Siebert (1979): *The Market for Labour: An Analytical Treatment*, Santa Monica, Calif.: Goodyear.

Aldcroft, D. (1967): 'Economic Growth in the Interwar Years: A Reassessment', *Economic History Review*, Vol. 20, No. 2.

Bailey, N. B. (1983): 'The Labor Market in the 1930s', in J. Tobin (ed.), *Macro-Economics, Prices and Quantities*, Oxford: Basil Blackwell.

Bakke, E. W. (1935): *Insurance or Dole*, New Haven, Conn.: Yale University Press.

Beenstock, M., and P. Warburton (1986a): 'Wages and Unemployment in Interwar Britain', *Explorations in Economic History*, Vol. 23, No. 2, April.

Beenstock, M., and P. Warburton (1986b): 'The Market for Labour in Interwar Britain', Discussion Paper No. 105, London: Centre for Economic Policy Research.

Benjamin, D., and K. Matthews (1990): 'Juvenile Unemployment and the School Leaving Age', Clemson, S. Carolina: Clemson University (mimeo).

Benjamin, D. (1989): 'A Comment on Crafts', South Carolina: Clemson University (mimeo).

Benjamin, D. K., and L. A. Kochin (1978): 'Unemployment and the Dole: The Evidence from Interwar Britain', in H.

Grubel (ed.), *International Evidence on the Effects of Unemployment Compensation*, Toronto: University of Toronto Press, pp. 303-18.

Benjamin, D. K., and L. A. Kochin (1979a): 'Searching for an Explanation of Unemployment in Interwar Britain'. *Journal of Political Economy*, Vol. 87, No. 3.

Benjamin, D. K., and L. A. Kochin (1979b): 'What Went Right with Juvenile Unemployment Policy between the Wars?: A Comment', *Economic History Review*, Vol. 32, No. 4.

Benjamin, D. K., and L. A. Kochin (1982): 'Unemployment and Unemployment Benefits in Twentieth Century Britain: A Reply to our Critics', *Journal of Political Economy*, Vol. 90, No. 2.

Beveridge, W. H. (1930): *The Past and Present of Unemployment Insurance*, Barnett House Papers No. 13, London: Oxford University Press.

Bowley, A. L. (1937): *Wages and Income since 1860*, Cambridge: Cambridge University Press.

Broadberry, S. (1982): 'Labour market models of the Great Depression', Queen's College, Oxford (mimeo).

Broadberry, S. N. (1983): 'Unemployment in Interwar Britain: A Disequilibrium Approach', *Oxford Economic Papers*, Vol. 34, Supplement.

Broadberry, S. (1986): 'Aggregate Supply in Interwar Britain', *Economic Journal*, Vol. 96, June.

Burns, E. M. (1941): *British Unemployment Programs 1920-1938*, Washington DC: Social Science Research Council.

Calvert, H. (1974): *Social Security Law*, London: Sweet and Maxwell.

Cannan, E. (1928): *An Economist's Protest*, New York: Adelphi.

Cannan, E. (1930): 'The Problem of Unemployment', *Economic Journal*, Vol. 40, March.

Capie, F., and A. Collins (1983): *The Interwar British Economy*, Manchester: Manchester University Press.

Casson, M. (1983): *Economics of Unemployment: An Historical Perspective*, Oxford: Martin Robertson.

Chapman, A., and R. Knight (1953): *Wages and Salaries in the United Kingdom 1920-1938*, London: Cambridge University Press.

Churchill, W. (1930): 'The Dole', *Saturday Evening Post*, 29 March, pp. 6-7.

Clark, C. (1932): *The National Income, 1924-1931*, London: Macmillan and Cass.

Clark, C. (1937): *National Income and Outlay*, London: Macmillan and Cass.

Clay, H. (1928): 'Unemployment and Wage Rates', *Economic Journal*, Vol. 38.

Clay, H. (1929a): *The Postwar Unemployment Problem*, London: Macmillan.

Clay, H. (1929b): 'The Public Regulation of Wages in Great Britain', *Economic Journal*, Vol. 39.

Cohen, P. (1938): *Unemployment Insurance and Assistance in Britain*, London: Harrap.

Collins, M. (1982): 'Unemployment in Interwar Britain: Still Searching for an Explanation', *Journal of Political Economy*, Vol. 90, No. 2.

Crafts, N. F. R. (1987): 'Long Term Unemployment in Britain in the 1930s', *Economic History Review*, Vol. 40, No. 3.

Cross, R. (1982): 'How much voluntary unemployment in Interwar Britain', *Journal of Political Economy*, Vol. 90, No. 2.

Cunliffe Committee (1919): *Committee on Currency and Foreign Exchange after the War*, Cmd. 9182, London: HMSO.

Darby, M. R. (1976): 'Three-and-half Million U.S. Employees have been Mislaid: or an Explanation of Unemployment, 1934-1941', *Journal of Political Economy*, Vol. 84, No. 1.

Deacon, A. J. (1976): *In Search of the Scrounger: The Administration of Unemployment Insurance in Britain 1920-1931*, London: Bell and Sons.

Department of Employment and Productivity (1971): *British Labour Statistics Historical Abstract 1886-1968*, London: HMSO.

Dimsdale, N. H., S. J. Nickell, and N. Horsewood (1989): 'Real Wages and Unemployment in Britain during the 1930s', *Economic Journal*, Vol. 99, No. 396, June.

Dimsdale, N. H. (1981): 'British Monetary Policy and the Exchange Rate', *Oxford Economic Papers*, Vol. 33, Supplement.

Douglas, P. H., and A. Director (1931): *The Problem of Unemployment*, New York: Macmillan.

Eichengreen, B. (1987a): 'Unemployment in Interwar Britain: Dole or Doldrums?', *Oxford Economic Papers*, Vol. 39, No. 4.

Eichengreen, B. (1987b): 'Juvenile Unemployment in Interwar Britain: The Emergence of a Problem', Discussion Paper No. 194, London: Centre for Economic Policy Research.

Feinstein, C. H. (1972): *National Income Expenditure and Output of the United Kingdom, 1855-1965*, Cambridge: Cambridge University Press.

Feldstein, M. (1976): 'Temporary Layoffs in the Theory of Unemployment', *Journal of Political Economy* Vol. 84, No. 5, October.

Friedman, M. (1967): 'The Monetary Theory of Henry Simons', *Journal of Law and Economics*, Vol. 10, October.

Friedman, M., and A. J. Schwartz (1963): *A Monetary History of the United States, 1867-1960*, Princeton, N.J.: Princeton University Press.

Friedman, M., and G. S. Becker (1957): 'A Statistical Illusion in Judging Keynesian Models', *Journal of Political Economy*, Vol. 65, No. 1, February.

Gilson, M. B. (1931): *Unemployment Insurance in Great Britain: The National System and Additional Benefit Plans*, New York: Industrial Relations Counselors.

Glynn, S., and J. Oxborrow (1976): *Interwar Britain: A Social and Economic History*, London and New York: Allen & Unwin.

Greenwood, W. (1933): *Love on the Dole*, Harmondsworth: Penguin Books, 1969.

Hancock, K. J. (1960): 'Unemployment and the Economists in the 1920s', *Economica*, Vol. 27, No. 108, November.

Hatton, T. (1980): 'Unemployment in Interwar Britain: A Role for the Dole', Unpublished manuscript.

Hatton, T. J. (1983): 'Unemployment Benefits and the Macroeconomics of the Interwar Labour Market', *Oxford Economic Papers*, Vol. 35, Supplement.

Hatton, T. J. (1988): 'A Quarterly Model of the Labour Market in Interwar Britain', *Oxford Bulletin of Economics and Statistics*, Vol. 50, No. 1, February.

Holden, K., and D. Peel (1986): 'The Impact of Benefits on Unemployment in Britain in the Interwar Period: Some Further Empirical Evidence', *Journal of Macroeconomics*, Vol. 8, No. 2, Spring.

Howson, S., and D. Winch (1977): *The Economic Advisory Council 1930-1939*, Cambridge: Cambridge University Press.

Irish, M., and D. Winter (1981): 'Did the Aggregate Market for Labour Clear in Interwar Britain?: Some Econometric Evidence', University of Bristol (mimeo).

Jackman, R., R. Layard, S. Nickell, and S. Wadwhani (1989): 'Unemployment', Centre for Labour Economics, London School of Economics (mimeo).

Kesselman, J., and N. Savin (1978): 'Three and a half million workers were never lost', *Economic Inquiry*, Vol. 16, April.

Keynes, J. M. (1930): *A Treatise on Money*, Vol. II, London: Macmillan.

Keynes, J. M. (1931): 'An Economic Analysis of Unemployment', in P. Q. Wright (ed.), *Unemployment as a World Problem: Lectures on the Harris Foundation 1931*, Chicago: University of Chicago Press.

Keynes, J. M. (1936): *The General Theory of Employment Interest and Money*, London: Macmillan.

Keynes, J. M. (1973): *The Collected Writings*, Vol. XIII, D. Moggridge (ed.), London: Macmillan, St Martins Press, for the Royal Economic Society.

Keynes, J. M. (1981): *The Collected Writings*, Vol. XX, D. Moggridge (ed.), London: Macmillan for the Royal Economic Society.

Lebergott, S. (1948): 'Labor Force Employment and Unemployment 1929-1939: Estimating Methods', *Monthly Labor Review*, Vol. 66, July.

Levacic, R. (1984): 'Keynes was a Monetarist', *Economic Affairs*, Vol. 4, No. 3, April-June.

Lucas, R. E., and L. A. Rapping (1972): 'Unemployment in the Great Depression: Is there a full explanation?', *Journal of Political Economy*, Vol. 80, No. 1, September/October.

Macmillan Committee (1931): *Committee on Finance and Industry*, Cmd. 3897, London: HMSO.

Matthews, K. G. P. (1986a): *The Interwar Economy*, Aldershot: Gower.

Matthews, K. G. P. (1986b): 'Was Sterling Overvalued in 1925?', *Economic History Review*, Vol. XXXIX, No. 4, November.

Matthews, K. G. P. (1987): 'Unemployment in Inter-war Britain: An Equilibrium Approach', *Bulletin of Economic Research*, Vol. 39, No. 2, April.

Matthews, K. G. P. (1989a): 'Was Sterling Overvalued in 1925? A Reply and Further Evidence', *Economic History Review*, Vol. XLII, No. 1, February.

Matthews, K. G. P. (1989b): 'Could Lloyd George Have Done It? The Pledge Re-examined', *Oxford Economic Papers*, Vol. 41, No. 2.

McClosky, D. N. (1983): 'The Rhetoric of Economics', *Journal of Economic Literature*, Vol. XXI, No. 2, June.

Metcalf, D., S. Nickell, and N. Floros (1982): 'Still Searching for an Explanation of Unemployment in Interwar Britain', *Journal of Political Economy*, Vol. 90, No. 2.

Mincer, J. (1974): *Schooling, Experience and Earnings*, New York: National Bureau of Economic Research.

Minford, A. P. L. (1983): 'Labour Market Equilibrium in an Open Economy', *Oxford Economic Papers*, Vol. 35, Supplement.

Minford, P., with P. Ashton, M. Peel, D. Davies, and A. Sprague (1985): *Unemployment: Cause and Cure* (2nd edn.), Oxford: Basil Blackwell.

Ministry of Labour (1929): *Standard Time Rates of Wages and Hours of Labour in Great Britain and Northern Ireland*, London: HMSO.

Ministry of Labour (1933): *Report on the Operation of the Anomalies Regulations, 3rd October 1931 to 29th April 1933*, Cmd. 4346, London: HMSO.

Ministry of Labour Gazette (various issues), London: HMSO, 1920-38.

Mitchell, B. R., and P. Deane (1962): *Abstract of British Historical Statistics*, Cambridge: Cambridge University Press.

Moggridge, D. (1969): *The Return to Gold 1925*, Cambridge: Cambridge University Press.

Morgan, E. V. (1952): *Studies in British Financial Policy 1914-1925*, London: Macmillan.

Ormerod, P., and G. D. N. Worswick (1982): 'Unemployment in Interwar Britain', *Journal of Political Economy*, Vol. 90, No. 2.

Oswald, A. J. (1982): 'The Microeconomic Theory of the Trade Union', *Economic Journal*, Vol. 92, September.

Pelling, H. (1973): *A History of British Trade Unionism* (2nd edn.), London: Penguin Books.

Pigou, A. C. (1927): 'Wage Policy and Unemployment', *Economic Journal*, Vol. XXXVII, No. 147, September.

Pigou, A. C. (1931): 'Evidence', in *Minutes of Evidence taken before the Committee on Finance and Industry*, Vol. II, London: HMSO.

Pilgrim Trust (1938): *Men Without Work*, Cambridge: Cambridge University Press.

Pollard, S. (1962): *The Development of the British Economy, 1914-1950*, London: Arnold.

Ramsbottom, E. C. (1935): 'The Course of Wage Rates in the United Kingdom, 1921-1934', *Journal of the Royal Statistical Society*, Vol. XCVIII.

Ramsbottom, E. C. (1938): 'Wage Rates in the United Kingdom, 1934-1937', *Journal of the Royal Statistical Society*, Vol. CI.

Ramsbottom, E. C. (1939): 'Wage Rates in the United Kingdom in 1938', *Journal of the Royal Statistical Society*, Vol. CII.

Reder, M. W. (1958): *Labor in a Growing Economy*, New York: Wiley.

Richardson, H. (1962): 'The Basis of Economic Recovery in the 1930s: A Review and a New Interpretation', *Economic History Review*, Vol. 15, No. 2.

Roback, J. (1982): 'Wages, Rents, and the Quality of Life', *Journal of Political Economy*, Vol. 90.

Rosen, S. (1979): 'Wage-based Indices of Urban Quality of Life', in P. Mieszkowski and M. Straszheim (eds.), *Current Issues in Urban Economics*, Baltimore: Johns Hopkins University Press.

Routh, G. (1980): *Occupation and Pay in Great Britain, 1906-79*, London: Macmillan.

Rowe, J. W. F. (1928): *Wages in Practice and Theory*, London: George Routledge & Sons.

Royal Commission (1932a): *Final Report of the Royal Commission on Unemployment Insurance*, Cmd. 4185, London: HMSO.

Royal Commission (1932b): *Appendices to the Minutes of Evidence. Final Report of the Royal Commission on Unemployment Insurance*, Cmd. 4185-II, London: HMSO.

Rueff, J. (1925): 'Les Variations du Chomage en Angleterre', *Revue Politique et Parliamentaire*, December.

Rueff, J. J. (1931): 'L'Assurance chomage cause du chomage permanent', *Revue Economique Politique*, Vol. 45, March/April.

Sayers, R. (1969): 'The Return to Gold, 1925', reprinted in S. Pollard (ed.), *The Gold Standard and Employment Policies*, London: Methuen.

Smyth, D. J. (1983): 'The British Labour Market in Disequilibrium: Did the Dole Reduce Employment in Interwar Britain?', *Journal of Macroeconomics*, Vol. 5, No. 1.

Steinbeck, J. (1951): *The Grapes of Wrath*, London: Penguin Books.

Stigler, G. J. (1961): 'The Economics of Information', *Journal of Political Economy*, Vol. 69.

Taylor, A. J. P. (1965): *English History, 1914-1945*, Oxford: Clarendon Press.

Unemployment Compensation Interpretation Service (1938): *Benefit Decisions of the British Umpire: A Codification and Text of Selected Decisions*, Benefit Series General Supplement No. 1, Social Security Board, Washington DC: Government Printing Office.

Unemployment Insurance in Great Britain: A Critical Examination by the Authors of 'The Third Winter of Unemployment' (1925): London: Macmillan.

US Bureau of the Census (1947): 'Labor Force, Employment and Unemployment in the United States, 1940 to 1946', *Labor Force Bulletin, Current Population Reports*, Series p-50, No. 2, Washington: Government Printing Office.

Wallis, J. (1989): 'Employment in the Great Depression: New Data and Hypotheses', *Explorations in Economic History*, Vol. 26, No. 1.

Wallis, J., and D. Benjamin (1981): 'Public Relief and Private

Employment in the Great Depression', *Journal of Economic History*, Vol. 41, No. 1.

Wells, W. (1983): 'The Relative Pay and Employment of Young People', Research Paper No. 42, London: Department of Employment.

Winch, D. (1969): *Economics and Policy: A Historical Study*, New York: Walker.

Published in 1992

OVERSEAS INVESTMENTS, CAPITAL GAINS AND THE BALANCE OF PAYMENTS

CLIFF PRATTEN

Since 1945, the United Kingdom's share of world manufacturing output has declined from an artificially high 25 per cent of world trade and had stabilised at just below 10 per cent by the late 1980s. The nature of exports has also changed, reflecting the decline in traditional industries such as steel and shipbuilding and the emergence of the knowledge-based industries such as financial services and electronics.

In this *Research Monograph* the balance of payments of the United Kingdom is thoroughly examined; the contribution of services such as banking, insurance and shipping has ensured that the balance of payments is in much better shape than is generally contended.

For example, capital gains on overseas investment since 1979, made possible by the abolition of exchange control, have made a contribution of more than four times the current account deficit over the corresponding period.

As recent international events have shown, the concept of the nation state is still alive. The ability to measure the effects of both outward and inward investment across national boundaries will be fundamental to understanding the economic strengths of each nation.

ISBN 0-255 36303-6　　Research Monograph 48　　**£7·95**

THE INSTITUTE OF ECONOMIC AFFAIRS
2 Lord North Street, Westminster
London SW1P 3LB　　Telephone: 071-799 3745

Published in 1992

Monetarism and Monetary Policy

ANNA J. SCHWARTZ

The emergence of monetarism as an alternative to orthodox Keynesian theory owes much to the pioneering work of Anna J. Schwartz. *A Monetary History of the United States, 1867-1960,* which she co-authored with Milton Friedman, has become a classic, and has changed the way in which economists study monetary policy and monetary history.

In this *Occasional Paper,* she examines the transformation from pegged to floating exchange rates, and assesses the behaviour of these rates in relation to monetary policy. Are they an appropriate objective of policy? Do they provide information about monetary conditions?

The sale or purchase of foreign currency by the monetary authorities has no demonstrable effect on the exchange market, apart from adding to the uncertainty of those who play the market, but it can distort domestic monetary growth and ultimately the price level.

Although the conclusions reached are largely, but not exclusively, based on her studies of the United States, they do have important policy implications for Britain and other countries. Monetary policy can stabilise the exchange rate *or* the price level – but not both.

ISBN 0-255 36302-8 Occasional Paper 86

The Institute of Economic Affairs
2 Lord North Street, Westminster
London SW1P 3LB
Telephone: 071-799 3745

£3.95